Cast Again

12.1.96

*For Shelly —
Because you have the
fishing spirit — all my best,
Jennifer Olsson*

Cast Again

JENNIFER OLSSON

Lyons & Burford, Publishers

Printed in the United States of America.

Design by LaBreacht Design

Drawings by Jennifer Lowe

10 9 8 7 6 5 4 3 2 1

Olsson, Jennifer
    Cast Again / Jennifer Olsson.
        p.   cm.
    ISBN 1-55821-442-9
    1. Trout Fishing—Montana—Anecdotes. 2. Fly fishing—Montana—Anecdotes. 3. Olsson, Jennifer. 4. Fishing guides—United States—Biography. 5. Women fishing guides—United States—Biography.
I. Title
SH688.U6058,   1996
799.1'2'-02—dc20
[B]
                                                                            96-303
                                                                            CIP

This book is dedicated to

my husband, Lars-Åke.

Your love keeps my spirit alive.

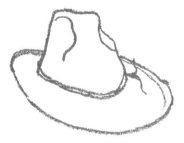

Contents

Acknowledgments

*T*hanks to my father, Jack Miller, who had the interest and the patience to take his daughters and sons fishing, and who selflessly gave us his time, encouragement, love, and knowledge. To Peter, who shares his mother with rivers. To my editor, Lilly Golden, who believed, encouraged, and helped make this dream come true.

I wish to thank my mother, Barbara, and my grandmothers, Erie and Alma. Their courage, strength, generosity, and wisdom continues to inspire. Their absence is felt daily.

And especially to Lars-Åke, whose commitment to us and this book made it possible. *Jag älskar dig.*

Preface

*O*n the first trip I ever guided, I forgot to pack my wading boots. While my two gentlemen clients changed into their waders, I searched through the tackle and duffel bags in the back of my Jeep to see where I might have put them. It became clear to me that I had left them on the back porch at home; a sudden and terrible sinking feeling hit me.

I remembered a story I once heard about acting with confidence. "You can eat salad with your fingers at the finest restaurant in the world if you act like you know what you're doing," I recalled. This helped; I would not mention anything about the missing boots to my clients. I would simply wade in in my shoes and jeans. The problem with this was that the shoes I had on were not mine, but a pair of brand-new loafers I had borrowed from a friend. As the reality of the cold creek water crept in through the seams of the polished leather, I wondered if I would still have clients or friends by the end of the day.

Had the two gentlemen not caught any fish or been difficult I might have hung up my wading staff that very day. But they caught several fish and were pleasant and kind, and my dream of teaching fly casting and fly fishing was greater than my embarrassment.

*M*y first impression of guides was gained as a teenager. My family and I would fish in Montana for a few weeks every summer—sometimes more—and at least once a year my father would hire a guide to float us down the Madison River. Like the religious on Sundays we rose to cast from bow and stern, and when the guide hollered for us to sit while he rowed the boat through rough or shallow waters, we sat in unison. I believed guides knew everything. They had certain inside information. Just having a guide choose the fly and tie it on convinced me that I would catch a trout on my next cast. I never wanted to disappoint or be a nuisance. When my fly got stuck in the willows and the guide rowed upstream to retrieve it, I felt great shame.

It never occurred to me that I could be a guide. And even later, when as a college student I got my first job working at Bud Lilly's Trout Shop in West Yellowstone, the inside world of fly fishing seemed to belong to men. The shop was divided into three sections: tackle, clothing, and art. I was hired to wait on the customers who wanted to buy a new shirt or watercolor.

The smell of pipe smoke and conversation about fishing floated past the waders and Elk Hair Caddis over to the long johns and hats where I could, on occasion, spy on the world of men and their desires to cast into the waters of Yellowstone Park, the Madison, the Gallatin, and the Henry's Fork. I could not join them in conversation, nor could I share with them my enthusiasm for a sport they sounded like they owned. I could only listen for fishing tips—which flies the fish were taking, which places trout were being found—while I helped customers find the right size.

But sometimes, if the guides were not too tired after their trips, or if they had a day off, I was invited to fish with them at their favorite places on the Henry's Fork or the upper Madison. It was the first time outside my family I felt accepted as a fly fisher. I began to believe I might be able to walk through the door that seemed to be for authorized personnel only.

Without my guide friends, or without a father who believed it was just as important to take his daughters fishing as it was his sons, feelings of being fenced out of the fly-fishing universe might have kept me away. But I also had another inspiration. When I was fifteen, a photograph of Joan and Lee Wulff on the wall of a small fly shop I visited caught my attention. "Who are they?" I asked, pointing to the autographed portrait. That was when I learned that they were professional fly fishers and that she was a fly-casting champion. There were possibilities after all.

Ten years later I owned a fly shop along with my first husband. It was a small shop, and we sold only flies and tackle, but I especially liked selling the fly rods. I could go outside with a strung rod and talk with someone about casting and fishing. I realized that this was what I wanted to do.

It was not long before I found myself checking luggage through to New York and carrying my rod case onto the plane. It was a pilgrimage: I needed to meet Joan, and to ask her to tell me if I was good enough. When I walked through the door of the Wulff School and saw her in person for the first time, I could not speak except to introduce myself. With a deep breath, I took a seat in the classroom. I was going to learn something there.

I arrived home full of enthusiasm and Joan's encouragement to become a fly-casting instructor and guide. I was going to teach people what I knew about trout fishing and take them to rivers and make them feel welcome there. Especially women, because historically they had been left out—either by choice or by habit—and when they wanted to begin with a rod and fly, they would need what I had needed when I started fly fishing: a good teacher who had patience and was someone they could relate to.

Since my first waderless guide trip I have guided many people to trout on a fly. As their guide, I lead them to water, choose their flies, talk them through the cast and presentation, untangle their leaders, and hope that trout will rise. I used to believe that a guide was a Dr. Doolittle with a fly rod. I know now that knowledge can improve one's luck, but serendipity leads us to fish more often than not, and inspires us to believe that something wonderful is just around the next bend. Getting tangled along the way is just part of the journey.

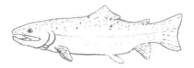

You Don't Look Like a Fishin' Guide

When I first saw Annie, who stood next to her husband in the lobby of the Holiday Inn, I thought, "Uh, oh. Southern Princess. Won't like the cold rainy weather. Will be uncomfortable outdoors. She'll stay in the car with a book."

Her nails were perfectly manicured and painted. She wore makeup. The scent of gardenia was in her perfume. Annie's southern drawl stretched one-syllable words into three and drew out the last word of every sentence until it dropped off her tongue from exhaustion.

"It's a pleasure to meet youuuuu. Youuuu don't look like a fishing guiiiiiiide."

Outside, a bolt of lightning flashed across the sky and thunder followed.

I have a feeling that when clients call me for the first time, they picture a woman in a log cabin whose living room is decorated with animal skins, a moose head, and wicker creels. Homemade soup is perpetually warming in a big kettle on the stove, and freshly baked bread comes out of the oven daily. Herbal tea is served. A faithful dog wearing a red bandanna sleeps on the Navajo rug in front of the fireplace, and likes to go for rides in the pickup. They imagine a big-bosomed, makeup-boycotting, Birkenstock-wearing free spirit. She lives to fly fish, to be one with nature.

They would be surprised to know that I live in a Montana suburb in a brown house complete with lawn mower and Weber grill. No pets. Soup comes out of a can. Bread comes from Safeway. Though I love to fly fish and be out in nature, I only dream about a log cabin on the banks of a trout stream.

I too create pictures of clients when they call. When Annie's husband, Dennis, called to book a trip with me, all I knew was that they were from the South, that Dennis had some experience, and that Annie had much less. The night before their trip, rain woke me at three in the morning. Like an unwanted visitor, the heavy rain drops rapped on the shingles of my house. "Go away," I murmured in the dark. I imagined a delicate, frowning, southern woman standing with wet hair beneath a rain-soaked hat. Taking a beginner out in wind and rain is a bad idea. Maybe they would cancel, I hoped.

At 7 A.M. I was in the kitchen packing the lunches we would need. Outside, a grouchy sky rumbled. There seemed to be no sign that the weather would improve.

*T*here they were in the hotel lobby, the handsome couple with green duffel bags, three rod tubes, and shirts with jumping trout over their right breast pockets. After introductions, Annie immediately said, "Now where's your car? Are you parked outside front?"

I reached to help carry bags and rod tubes and we headed for the parking lot. Before leaving the building, Annie whipped a clear plastic rain hat out of her pocket, the kind that comes folded like a Japanese fan, and snapped it open. She placed it gently over her head, tied the plastic strings beneath her chin, and followed me out.

"I know I look like I have a sandwich bag over my head, but I just had my hair duuune."

Dennis smiled and looked pleased.

The wipers flipped water off the windshield. Annie's conversational patter matched the raindrops that drummed on the roof of the Jeep. She quizzed me. What was my marital status? Children? What did my family think of my guiding career? Was I from Montana?

I told her that my grandparents were Montanans, but that I had grown up in Southern California.

"Jennifer, you're a real frontier woman! Coming all the way out here to start a fishing business."

I studied the horizon and looked for patches of blue, any sign that the rain might let up.

"Annie," I said, "I just want to let you know that if you don't want to get out in this rain, I can work with Dennis until it clears up."

"I'll be just fine. I brought my rain jacket."

I thought that she was a little naive. I was certain that as soon as she felt how cold and wet the world was outside the warm toaster-oven interior of my Jeep, she would recoil, pull out a good book, and tell us to have a good time.

The first thing I heard after I shut off the ignition was the sound of her door slamming. Annie jumped out and dashed to the back of the car to get at her fishing gear.

"Better get these waders on. Dennis, I need my rain jacket. Jennifer, do you think I should put on an extra sweater? I brought one just in case."

Bags were unzipped, clothing and neoprene sprang out. Like a well-rehearsed drill team, Annie and Dennis stepped into their waders, boots, sweaters, socks, and rain gear effortlessly. I hopped around on one foot, trying to get on my last boot, while they stood in front of me fully suited, holding rigged fly rods, waiting for instructions.

Annie marched ahead and led us down the trail. Dennis and I walked calmly behind her like two old gentleman.

"You go on and fish with Annie. She's been looking forward to this for a long time," said Dennis. "I'll fish here for a while."

Dennis separated from me, crashed through some dog-wood brush, and disappeared over the bank into the river.

"Wait, Annie," I called out.

I had to jog to catch up.

Annie turned to wait for me on the trail: fresh lipstick, rain dripping off her plastic hat, smile as big as the meadow we were in. I had been wrong. This was *not* a Southern princess. This was a Southern Woman.

I am more careful now when a client calls me from places like Tennessee, Georgia, or Mississippi. When she says, "Hello, this is Sue Ellen, my husband and I are coming out to fish with you. We're just so excited we can hardly stand it. What I called for was to find out if I should bring an extra sweater. I hear it gets chilly in the evenings there," I picture a debutante who has had her hair done to go fishing. She will notice what other women in the area are wearing and will comment on houses that have some style. But I do not let her fool me. Pouring rain, thunder, and lightning will not keep her from the outdoors. She grew up fishin' with her daddy. She makes fishing guides look tired. I think, book her—plan to learn how to smile in the rain.

I'd Like to Get My Wife into Fly Fishing

I could tell we were not off to a good start. Billie sat quietly in her seat as we backed out of the motel's driveway. Her husband waved good-bye enthusiastically and shouted, in his Tennessee drawl, "You girls have a good time now!"

I waved back at him. Billie did not.

My Jeep smelled like a fly shop, formaldehyde, and smoked cigarettes. We had just loaded Billie's birthday gifts, still fresh in their boxes, into the back: new waders, wading boots, fishing vest, long johns, rain jacket, fly rod and reel. It was all top-of-the-line gear. None of it had she ever used.

This was not the first time I had been called to the rescue. Many times my phone rings and a polite gentleman on the other end says, "I'd like to get my wife into fly fishing."

I have always been sympathetic to this wish and found it rather endearing.

"Has she had any experience?" I ask.

"Well, I've been fly fishing for years. I've tried to teach her in the past, but it was a disaster. I know she'd like it if she went with you."

I take his name and address, and suggest a few available dates. We meet three months later and he is left waving after my dusty taillights as I drive his darling off to clear blue waters. Anxiously, like a patient waiting for the pathology report, he waits for our return.

When my car arrives in the driveway at the end of a long day he runs out to see if she, like an emerging mayfly, has made a transformation. He wants to know how we did, how many we caught, is she any good, did she like it? Little does he know that during the course of the day I have not only been instructing his wife in the fine art of fly casting, I have heard the whole story of their marriage. He cannot cook, he is too hard on their son, and his parents were alcoholics.

They hug and kiss when she steps out of the car, and I report, "We had a great time. Yes, she did just fine. We caught three fish, and one was over fifteen inches. Her casting needs more practice, but she knows what to work on. Let her go at her own pace."

Unfortunately, in this case, Billie had been the last to know about her birthday trip, and I felt I was getting some of the blame. I began to chat about the weather and how I had picked out a place for us to fish and packed our lunch when suddenly she patted my shoulder with her manicured hand. With well-rehearsed southern charm, she informed me that we would not be going fishing.

"Jennifer, I think that you are just so sweet and good to come out here and take me fishing, and I really like you, but I have tried and tried and I do not like to fish. I know Hamilton wants me to fish, but I am just not interested. What I really want to know is where did you get that cute little cowboy hat?"

I parked outside the local western shop where I had bought my hat a few years back and we sashayed in. Billie tried on hat after hat. This brim was too wide, that crown was too high, this color was not what she wanted. Then, she found a tan outback hat that was just right. I warned her that it was not western, it was Australian, but she had seen cowboys on TV wearing the type so it did not matter. She examined all of the horsehair hatbands and stampede strings and put her choices on the counter. Then we moved to the clothing department. Jeans, blouses, duster coats, cowboy boots. I stood outside the dressing room and called out sizes to the salesperson who scurried back and forth between us and the racks.

"We need this in a size twelve, and this in a ten."

It occurred to me that women's sizes were the same as hook sizes. I was guiding after all.

"Here, you can put this back." Catch-and-release. "Now *that* you have to have!" Rising trout. "Oh, this is gorgeous, you should try it on." Casting. "I don't know which one to get." Knots and tangles. "I'll get them both." Knots untangled.

Boxes and bags and two hours later we left for lunch. My Jeep looked like a UPS truck. After our shopping safari, Billie's attitude improved greatly. Examining herself in the passenger-side mirror, she reapplied lipstick.

"I am so glad we found this hat. I have always wanted one. It's a color you can wear with everything. All that western stuff is so popular now. I feel like I have a little souvenir from Montana."

My plan was to keep her happy and to try, at some point, to coax her into the water. First, a picnic on the Madison River.

"Oh, this is lovely! What cute little napkins. Did you make them yourself? Oh, I'll have a Coke, thank you. I can't possibly eat this whole sandwich, I'll just eat half. You know how it is when you're on vacation. I don't think I've seen a vegetable the entire time I've been here."

It occurred to me that this trip had taken on a life of its own. The mystic waters of the Madison that said "come in!" to me, said nothing to her. She smiled at the river as it danced just beyond her feet, and that was all.

"What do you think about trying on some of your birthday presents?" I suggested.

"Well, I guess I should."

"I can help you put your gear together, show you what's what."

"That would be lovely, but now, Jennifer, don't expect too much. I've never been very good at this."

"We'll take it slow."

Waders, socks, boots, suspenders, fishing vest, new hat, fly rod and reel later, Billie followed me down to the river's edge. Holding her arm and leading her, I said, "Let's step in here."

One foot followed the other.

"Good, Billie. How does it feel?"

"It feels fine. Why don't you fish for a while and I'll watch. I learn by watching."

"Okay. I'll make a few casts and you can see how to fish this area in front of you."

Billie watched. I fished. We were both happy with the arrangement. I hooked fish for her, and she reeled them in.

"Oh, that's a nice one," Billie said as I held our catch in my hands. "Now, what is that? It doesn't look like a rainbow. A brown trout, I've never seen a brown trout before. I think rainbows are so pretty. Don't you?"

I thought she might be getting interested after all.

"Do you want to try and cast now?"

"Well, just a few. . . . Oh, it's not going very far."

"It doesn't have to. You're casting far enough."

"Are you joking? My husband can cast it way over there to the other bank."

"You're doing it just right for you. You can't compare yourself to anyone else. Make this sport what you want. You only have to be what you want to be."

Billie wanted to be alone and insisted I go downstream. Twenty minutes later she wanted to leave.

"This has been wonderful. I'd like to quit now. I'm a little tired."

In a way, I felt we had succeeded. Her wading boots were wet, she had reeled in a few fish, and she had spent a few minutes casting. We had something to report. Hamilton and Billie would have something to discuss at dinner.

The hum of the car traveling along the straight, broad road to town put Billie to sleep. She dozed up to the city limits of West Yellowstone with her head lolled back and her mouth hung open. I had to assure her she had not been snoring.

"All that fresh air and sunshine must have tired me out," she said, straightening her clothes and hat.

"Billie, I don't mean to be nosy or anything, but can I ask you a question?"

"Certainly."

"What are you going to do with the shopping bags?"

"Honey, I have been hiding shopping bags since before you were born."

Billie unbuckled herself and climbed into the backseat, where she separated clothes from shopping bags and stuffed them into the wader box. Next, she tucked belts and belt buckles down the legs of the waders, and put the cowboy boots in the wading shoe box.

"You can shove the bags under the front seats if you like, and I'll take care of them when I get home," I offered.

"Thank you, I will."

I heard the crumpling of paper, like someone wadding up newspaper to start a fire, and it was done. Billie climbed

back into her seat, flipped down the passenger-side mirror, and reapplied lipstick.

"Jennifer, I've had a very nice time. Thank you
so much."

"Billie, I had fun too. If you ever have any questions
about fishing or want to go shopping. . . . "

"You'll be the first person I'll call."

I helped Billie carry her boxes and gear up to the motel
room. Hamilton was not there.

That fall, I heard that Hamilton and Billie had bought
property and a house on the Madison. They had new car-
peting delivered in a semitruck. Billie called to ask how to
get in touch with an interior decorator. "I want to have the
house decorated like a fishing lodge. Log tables, willow
furniture, Indian rugs, craft shades on the lamps!" I gave
her the name of my friend who has a business in town.

Hamilton called in late October to ask me what kind
of new equipment he should get Billie for Christmas. He
said she liked to fish now. He said he could tell because
she had been ordering a lot lately from the Orvis catalog.

Just One

"You were out all day and only caught one trout?" her boyfriend, Norman, had said to her.

Actually, I had caught it and Molly had reeled it in, and it was not even a trout, it was a whitefish. It had been the first day of her first fly-fishing trip. In a way, I felt the same as Norman did—disappointed. I wanted Molly to catch more fish. I thought catching more fish would help her confidence. I felt I would fail her if we did not do better the next day.

For nearly a year, Molly and I had talked off and on over the phone before she announced that she and Norman, a financial consultant, would fly to Montana from their home in Southern California for a long weekend. He would stay in the motel to catch up on work. We would have two days to fish. She had been more than excited.

In preparation for the trip, Molly had joined a small fly-fishing club where the retired gentlemen members had been happy to demonstrate for her the correct methods of slinging a fly line backward and forward. They met every Sunday morning. It was their church. When Molly told the club she was planning to meet me and go after rainbows and browns in Montana, they were delighted, they were thrilled. She was a pilgrim leaving for the promised land. Flies were tied for her, advice was given, maps were drawn, and everyone was eager for her to hurry and go, and come back. She could give a talk about it at the next club meeting. She could write about it in the next newsletter. They just knew she would love it. They knew she would catch fish.

"Take lots of pictures, Molly," they begged her.

I pictured them waving and blowing kisses as she stepped onto the ramp that led to the plane.

"Yes," she sighed, as we loaded her gear into the back of my Jeep for our second day of fishing. "He just doesn't understand after everything he's heard about Montana and the fishing why we only caught one fish. He used to take charters and fish out on the ocean and he caught hundreds of fish a day. I don't think he's fished for trout much."

Knowing I had to make something happen, I had made plans to take Molly to a place I called Secret Creek. On this creek, ten- to twelve-inch rainbows hid behind every rock and took big Royal Wulffs and Parachute Adams without hesitation. This was the creek I went to when I wanted to immerse myself in nature and in solitude. I had told her the night before that she should prepare herself for a hike along a trail that wound through fragrant pines. I explained that we had to get an early start because it was a long drive and we would be back late. I had promised her lots of fish.

But there was a problem. I had to make a change in plans.

"Molly, I've changed my mind about where we will fish. We are going to drive up toward Big Sky and fish the Gallatin River."

Silence.

"Why?" she asked, sounding as if a box of chocolates had just been yanked from her grasp.

"I called over to a fly shop in the valley and talked to one of the guides about the creek, and he said it wasn't fishing very well."

This was a half-truth. I had spoken to the guide, but it had been a month earlier. What drove me away from my promised plan was something I did not think I could talk about right then.

The truth was, the entire evening before I had been having a strong feeling against going to the creek. It was a nagging, scary feeling that I kept bumping into in the hallway, the kitchen, and the shower.

It was fall, and there had been a number of bear sightings. I reasoned that I was thinking too much about the sign at the trail head to Secret Creek that read DANGER YOU ARE IN GRIZZLY COUNTRY. I tried to be reasonable and told myself, "In the morning the sun will come up and you will feel better, and you will want to go to the creek." But I cowered under my covers in my dark room.

When I woke up I was still struggling with my desire to go and a force that demanded I not. I was being pushed off my creek and pulled upstream onto the Gallatin River and I could not understand why. The Gallatin had been fishing lousy for weeks. Why would I suddenly want to go to the Gallatin? What kind of a guide was I?

"It's a beautiful drive," I assured her, but I did not have any comforting words for myself. I watched the steel-cold waters of the Gallatin tumble toward us as we followed the road upstream.

Molly recovered quickly, and the idea of fishing the Gallatin seemed to have become an acceptable change of plan. I pulled into an unmarked fishing access and took a rutted road toward a parking place near the river. Coffee from the thermos, and fingerless gloves, helped us fight off the morning frost. The sun was slow to stretch up over the top of the canyon walls. We were early. The other fly fishers who would arrive later were just ordering pancakes at a local café, or sleeping in. We would start the fishing with a lesson in nymphing techniques. A nine-foot 5X leader, one split-shot attached a foot above a size 12 Prince Nymph, and a bright pink piece of yarn tied in near the butt section as a strike indicator. The river washed against our neoprene legs as we stood together, client and guide, and seemed to take all my doubts downstream as we approached the first pool.

I demonstrated and instructed and stood over Molly like a stage mother. "Don't false-cast, just pick it up and cast it in. Mend, mend again. Keep your eye on the strike indicator. If it stops suddenly or jumps, lift your rod tip and strike. Fish from the top of the pool all the way through. Fish the other side of it as well. Fish the tail end of the pool where the riffled water begins. Strip line. Strip in more. You have too much line out. Fish your nymph closer. When your strike indicator is dragging in the water, your nymph is probably dragging too. Don't stare at it when it's dragging. Pick it up and cast again. Don't fish the same spot over and over again. Put your cast in another place. Good. Perfect. Beautiful. You're doing great, Molly!"

We settled into a rhythm of instruction and follow-through. As if with well-rehearsed dance steps that did not require counting out loud or staring at feet, Molly began to fish the nymph, and a nice, easy silence followed.

It had been quiet for several minutes while I watched her work the pool. The strike indicator suddenly charged upstream and I screamed, "Strike!" Molly reacted as if someone had jumped out of her bedroom closet in the middle of the night. We were both screaming. We must have screamed loud enough to send that and every other trout in the pool all the way down to the Missouri. The line went slack.

"I felt something! I felt something! Was that a fish?"

"Yes, it was," I laughed.

"Something pulled when I pulled up."

"Good. That's really good. We're getting closer."

Molly was persistent. Back again into the pool went the Prince Nymph. Several more casts and *wham!*, the biggest whitefish of the year grabbed the fly and shook, and shimmied, and tugged, and seemed just as relieved as we were when it finally fell into my net.

"Molly, you did that all by yourself. You did a great job. Great! Just great!"

"I saw the strike indicator and everything. I can't believe it!"

She was delighted with her developing skills. Then she asked, "What is a whitefish exactly?"

For some reason, I felt like someone who was caught in a lie.

"Whitefish are native to Montana and were here when Lewis and Clark came through. They're distant relatives of the trout."

I wanted to sound positive.

"Okay, the next one will be a trout," I promised.

We walked downstream and fished the run below the pool. We fished the area around the deadfall. We fished against the opposite bank. We fished the dark water, the fast water, and the shallow water. We changed the fly. We changed it back. Finally, I had Molly fish a strip of dark water against the opposite bank.

The sun was up almost in its noontime position. Shadows still fell on the water in front of us, but they were shrinking quickly. The clear, sunny sky would almost guarantee the end of the fishing for the day. The Gallatin does not fish well under clear skies. I wished for clouds. I looked at my watch. I was just getting ready to reprimand myself for not using my good sense, for not being a good guide, when it happened.

In an instant, all the shadows of the morning brightened as the strike indicator tore upstream and a trout, a very large trout, leapt from the depths of the river and slapped the water on its way back in.

"It's not a whitefish. It's not a whitefish," I yelled.

"What do I do, What do I do?" Molly yelled back.

"Get your hands off the line get your hands off the line get your hands off the line. Let him run let him run let him run!" I shouted out of nervousness and insistence that she hear me, and in her panic she tried to hand me the rod.

"No, no, no, it's your fish, it's your fish! You're going to be fine. I'll talk you through this."

I was shaking. The trout surged downstream and stopped. When a big fish that is running for its life stops unexpectedly, I always feel some alarm. Either it has found a rock to hide behind, or the fly has slipped out of its mouth and is caught on a tree root.

Taking Molly's arm, I carefully escorted her out of the deeper water and closer to the bank, where she could negotiate the trout into quiet water.

"Keep even tension on the line and rod tip. If he wants to run, take your hand off the reel. When he stops, start reeling again and put a little pressure on him to keep him from resting. If he goes to the left, try to steer him to the right. If he comes straight at you, grab the line and strip it in as fast as you can. Just be careful how much pressure you put on him. Now, slowly, start to reel."

Click, Click, Click.

The sound of the reel can be the loneliest sound in the world.

Click, Click, Click.

Movement and life reappeared at the end of the line. It made several zigzag dashes, came toward us, and stopped twenty feet in front.

"Take it easy, now, Molly, he won't like it when he sees me. Be ready to let him run. I'm going to go to the right and see if I can't get into position to net him. Easy pressure."

The moment was fragile. Air was scarce. I had to wait until the trout slowed and its movements told me it was ready. It paused briefly just to my left. I slipped the net under the water and popped it back up with our creature cupped in its cotton mesh: heavy, bent, and wet. River water dripped off my elbow. I felt like a midwife who had just delivered a baby.

"He's a brown! He's the biggest brown trout I have ever seen on this river!" I shouted. We hooted and hollered. It was Molly's first trout.

I ran to the car to retrieve her camera. If anyone had seen me dashing up the path back to the car, they would have known there was some kind of emergency. What is it about catching fish that makes you run, not walk? Makes you sing out your surprise in a shout or a smile? Something appears in your voice or in your face that was not there before the fish took your fly. Joy, fear, wonder, and the world seems to spin around the fish and you, new again.

I wish the club could have seen her. New mother, prom queen, little girl; holding her child, her flowers, her straight-A report card, her dream come true. Holding it above the water over the net, she was shining with happiness. They would have been so proud. I could hear them cheer and applaud.

We released the brown, after noting that it was a female. A female trout seemed appropriate for the moment as well.

We ate a picnic lunch on the bank overlooking the river—the river drenched in sunshine. Catching more fish did not seem to hold our interest. We lingered on the bank and stared into the water, wondering about our experience and the mystery we had witnessed.

If I am allowed to believe in such things as premonitions, then I guess I believe Molly was not supposed to go to my little creek and catch lots of small fish; she was supposed to go to the Gallatin and catch an eighteen-inch brown trout. I was supposed to get her there.

I hoped Norman could be happy for her. Would he stand with arms folded across his chest, reading glasses in one hand, wearing an expression of shock, saying, "What? Only one?"

"Tell Norman how well you did. Tell him it was like getting money back after taxes or picking a stock that doubles in value."

"I will," she said, and her smile told me that she would.

In the rearview mirror I saw Molly carrying her rods and gear into the motel lobby. The car was quiet and smelled of dampness and wet waders. I backed out of the parking spot and started for home.

"Secret Creek. I wonder how it's fishing after all?" I said to myself. No strange feeling tugged at my conscience as I pictured the hike along the pine-scented trail.

Tarpon Child

"*B*e ready at five-thirty," said my guide, before he hung up.

I waited in the early-morning darkness outside the motel until the headlights of a small, rusted pickup announced his arrival. My guide, or as they are properly called in the Keys—captain, had bushy gray eyebrows that reminded me of my father's. I could trust him.

We were going to fish for tarpon. People had gotten excited when they heard I was taking this trip. They gave me books and lots of advice, just like they did when, a year and a half earlier, I had announced that I was pregnant.

Tarpon fishing was going to be different than fishing for trout. I was told that Keys guides yelled foul things at you if you blew your casts or could not follow their directions; plus you had to bring the lunch. One person made a point of telling me that if I felt the hair rise on my arm, and my rod began to hum, I should throw it down because I was about to get hit by lightning. Everyone who had caught a tarpon said that it was the most exciting fishing they had ever experienced, but that I might go an entire week and not catch a thing.

My friend Mary, who had fished for tarpon before, said that after you have been out fishing in the hot and humid atmosphere of the Keys for six hours, all you want to do when you get back to shore is hide in a dark closet with a cold, wet towel over your face. That and pee.

"You'll lose your place on the flats if the captain has to take you all the way back to shore, so wear a bathing suit so that you can dip yourself in the ocean next to the boat. Either that or ask the captain to turn around while you pee in the bail bucket," she said.

Her warning got my attention. No liquids.

With all this good advice I thought I was prepared. We parked at Bud 'n' Mary's Marina and I followed my captain along the wooden dock to his boat. There was a lot of activity at the marina. Guides tended to their skiffs; clients organized gear, rubbed in sunscreen, and paced. I figured people liked getting up early in the Keys.

"You'll be fishing during the Men's Invitational Gold Cup Tournament," my captain explained.

It meant that twenty-five competitive male anglers would be tarpon fishing that week in the same area we would be. They were vying to win an inscription on the cup, and collect the paintings, the donated prizes, and the thousands in cash from the betting pool going on on the side. Even the guides won prizes if their clients placed.

The best guides had been hired a year earlier. Everyone had something to gain or lose. Guides did not speak or look at each other; participants, with an air of forced casualness, tried to appear as though it were just another day of fishing. No one discussed where tarpon had been seen the day before, when tournament fishers and their guides had been out scouting. Only the wakes of their boats after the starting gun went off would tell where they might be headed. But the starting gun would not fire until 6:30 A.M., and since we were not in the tournament we could leave before that. Our engine puttered in reverse as we backed away from the dock; solemn faces turned toward us. No one wished us luck.

Beyond the no-wake zone my captain pushed the throttle forward, and the warm Keys wind blew hard across our bodies. Thirty minutes later we stopped, and my captain anchored the boat by roping us into his poling stake. The boat rolled gently with the waves.

I was handed a 10-weight rod with a floating line matched to a Billy Pate reel. I stood on the bow as my guide showed me how to strip off line and let it fall in loops next to my feet.

"Leave the line the way it falls. That way it won't tangle," he cautioned.

This method would give me a head start on the quick roll-cast I would need to get line out fast enough. I stood ready with line and rod, holding a 3/0 tarpon fly called a Cockroach.

The boat dipped from side to side. I stood with feet apart and balanced myself with the rhythmic rocking. We were on the Atlantic side of the Keys, which tends to be rougher water than what is known as the bay side, or the backcountry. Choppy water is desirable, just as it is in trout fishing, because beneath a mottled surface the fish feel less vulnerable and do not spook as easily.

Mary had said the best part of tarpon fishing is when they jump. Jumps in tarpon fishing count. Landing a tarpon is, of course, ideal, but if you hook a tarpon and it jumps before breaking off, that is considered something of a victory. When you get back to the dock and someone asks, "How'd you do?" you can report your score by saying, "I jumped three and landed one."

I asked my guide about the best day he ever had. He said, "We jumped eight and landed six." These numbers made something else clear. Tarpon are hard to catch.

Two hours passed. I was offered soft drinks. I refused. I was offered the cooler as a bench to wait on until tarpon came by. I refused. I wanted to be ready when they came.

I studied the ocean bottom a dozen feet beneath me. Shades of yellow green, dark green, and darker green defined depth, plant life, sandy bottoms. Tarpon migrate in groups across this map. Their backs camouflage them against the dark green patches in the shallow water. Staring at the water, I wondered how many tarpon had snuck by us without notice.

Mary had encouraged me to stand barefoot on the bow so I could feel the line with my feet and not step on it during my cast. My feet became so hot on the white deck that I had to curl my toes and shift my weight from one foot to the other. Stubbornly, I remained standing, feet pink and sore from the heat, waiting with resolve for my chance to see the underwater birds fly by.

At the stern, the captain dipped an engine-oil-stained towel into the ocean, wrung it out, and threw it at my feet.

"Stand on that," he ordered as it slapped into my heels.

I accepted. The distracting pain subsided.

A stingray hovered near the sandy bottom, its wings softly undulating in a water breeze. Schools of mackerel jumped suddenly from the surface like popcorn. "Holy mackerel!" I joked. A gull screeched its nervous call from above, sounding like a bagpipe someone was squeezing the air out of. Like a prairie, the ocean looked flat and dull, but the longer I meditated on the sky and sea, the more absorbed I became by the constant movement and play of birds and sea creatures. I realized that I could have overlooked this other world. The one I could not see from Route 1, the highway that runs 106 miles from Key Largo to Key West. I wondered what else I had missed in my dash through life.

The people attracted to this mystic wilderness—people who came to the Keys to live and fish tarpon year after year—know more about weather patterns, tides, and phases of the moon than they do about the balance in their checkbook. Before the turn of the century, people went after tarpon in canoes. The first recorded tarpon hooked on a rod and reel came in 1882. As the tarpon was brought alongside the canoe, the fisherman, not even certain what he had caught, gaffed it. The gaff was built to hold a fifty-pound shark but, being too weak for the tarpon, it straightened, and the fisherman fell backward out of the boat. This event inspired the construction of lines, reels, and sturdy eight-foot-length bamboo rods that would hold a dancing, thrashing tarpon. Anglers began to keep a bucket of water in the boat; ladles of it were poured over the reel to cool it when it spun hot with the friction of a tarpon's run.

They also began to use hand-held harpoons. After the tarpon had been speared, the fisherman played it on the harpoon line by hand while the tarpon shook its massive head, leapt, or towed the boat behind it.

Even then it was considered a breach of "ethics" to kill any but your first tarpon. The meat of a tarpon has never been considered entrée quality, and the fish is too big for more than one to be hauled around in a canoe, anyway. Tarpon were precious as sport fish, but they were released.

For a release to count, the tarpon had to be hauled all the way into the canoe and then pushed back into the water. Sometimes after a long day it was agreed that a tarpon could be released next to the boat. It was a dangerous sport: In the process of wrestling with fish that could weigh as much as 100 pounds, fishermen were often dispatched over the side of their craft, and their canoes were easily swamped. Sometimes a fisherman who leaned over to unhook an exhausted tarpon was surprised by a shark who opened wide and bore down, tearing away the tarpon in a bloody froth.

On occasion, tarpon-fishing expeditions commenced from large cruising vessels that were anchored at a central location from which the canoes were launched. Camping trips into the backcountry were common. In those days the mangroves were unadulterated by human development, and new, pristine waters could be investigated while shorebirds called, the shy manatee slipped quietly away, and the tarpon rolled to the surface for a breath of ocean air. Today, wakes from speeding boats would probably swamp a canoe. And Jetskiers zoom like human mosquitoes through the flats—reminders that the intimate experience with water and tarpon was long ago.

The heat continued to swell and embrace. The sun was ruthless. Guides are riddled with scars left by dermatologists who have taken away "growths." The sunscreen's magic veil works well except when you miss a spot, usually in the shape of a quotation mark or comma. The marks burn themselves into the second layer of skin if you do not catch them by early afternoon. You wear your burn marks the rest of the week, as if giant typewriter keys have struck you in the neck or on the back of your leg.

My guide did not say much. It was too hot. Monosyllables worked best in the thick air.

At about 10 A.M. the sound of a racing motor charged toward us and then stopped 150 feet to our right. Since we had gotten there first, custom dictated that we park in the number-one position—the spot where the tarpon were expected to come by. This boat positioned itself at the number-two post. The captain staked his boat, the angler took several casts off the bow, and they settled in. Thirty minutes later, a third boat roared up and pulled in behind boat number two. It hung close behind boat number two, motor idling, rolling in the waves.

At first we could hear the conversation. From his platform, the second-position captain turned around to listen to what the client of the third boat was saying. Like the wind, the conversation shifted, agitated voices banged against one another. Hands waved dramatically. Then the voice of the guide in boat number two was raised loud enough for us to hear.

"Listen asshole, I don't care if you're in the goddamn Gold Cup. I'm not moving. Get out of here!"

He waved them away with the back of his hand. Away they went, moving carefully another 300 feet to the right, into the number-three position. A heated conversation continued in boat number two as the insult was reviewed, reexamined, and discussed. Its occupants glared over at boat number three, giving the message they were not going to easily forget the incident.

My captain chuckled to himself. "That's why I don't fish the tournaments anymore. Everyone takes themselves too seriously. I just like fishin'. Competition ruins it," he said quietly.

"Have you fished a lot of tournaments?" I asked.

"I used to do it all the time. Won a couple of them. Won it with Billy Pate once. But not anymore. I don't believe in them. No, I just like fishin'."

A small shark crossed in front of our boat. It gave my captain the opportunity to tell me how dangerous the big ones were. "There was a woman who loved to tarpon fish. She came out every year and fished for two and three weeks at a time. She was pretty good. Well, she had a tarpon on and was working it in when suddenly it charged the boat. The tarpon came out of the water and into the boat and right behind it was a hammerhead shark. The hammerhead came out of the water and slammed its head down on the side of the boat, knocking the tarpon out. The boat almost flipped over, but they were lucky. I guess she was laughing at first, but then she got hysterical. Couldn't stop crying. The captain took her back to the dock. I haven't seen her around. I don't think she fishes any more."

Thoughts about sharks jumping into your boat, like thoughts about grizzlies attacking you while you fish in Yellowstone Park, have to be examined in a brightly lit room, preferably in the kitchen at home. At any other time they need to be left behind, along with thoughts about plane crashes, car wrecks, and drive-by shootings.

"It must have really flipped her out," my captain offered as his final comment.

Creaks and groans from the boat, the breeze pushing past, the slap of water against the hull, a motor in the distance. The sounds of my captain shuffling across the platform at the stern in laceless tennis shoes. His heavy breathing when he poled the boat to another position. The sound of him hitching rope around the stake to keep us from drifting. The sounds were small, our talk was minimal, we seemed to be shrinking in this great expanse of water.

"Tarpon one o'clock!" His voice crashed the silence and I jumped.

"Forty feet," he shouted.

Miragelike torpedo shapes moved toward us. I had been told that tarpon spook easily, and I cringed at the noise my line made when it hit the water. I followed my captain's instructions as his voice rolled over my shoulders.

"Wait. Wait. Strip. Strip. Strip. Strip a little faster. He's got it!"

I was surprised by the take. It felt like someone gently tugging my elbow. I set the hook. Something the size of a bus pulled back.

"Hit 'im again."

I blasted myself into reverse and yanked on the line, trying to drive the sharpened hook in as deeply as possible. A ferocious pull forced me to push the rod forward and give line—like giving a horse the reins when riding down a steep hill. Slack line that had been hanging in front of the reel whipped back on my arm with a sting and shot arrow-straight out the guides of my rod. Speeding tarpon, line, and fly headed out to sea, and I was supposed to hold onto a crumbling cork grip and pull the beast back in.

Then it jumped. Before it jumped the tarpon surged like a gymnast charging the springboard before vaulting into space. Mary had said you have to bow to the tarpon when it jumps. I did not ask her at the time if the bow was a rite made in honor of the great fish, or if it was a particular move you had to make to keep the fish from breaking off. As in childbirth, I figured I would have time to ask any last-minute questions when I got to the hospital, and as in childbirth, there was no time to ask questions. The tarpon, its silver scales the size of dinner plates, rose up out of the ocean and shook its head. It was the eyes of the fish that left me paralyzed. Its big eyes seemed to recognize me.

I pointed my rod at the tarpon and bowed at the waist, the Japanese people do in greeting. My fish dropped back into the water, surged again, and sprang into the air, its head shaking, telling me "no!" I bowed again as the creature shook and danced and splashed on reentry.

I felt weak. My captain stepped up to the bow to watch. When the tarpon jumped again and I greeted it Asian-style, he asked calmly, "What are you doing?"

"I'm bowing to the tarpon."

Polite as he was, he still had to laugh.

"Who told you to do that?"

"My friend Mary said. . . ."

"No, not like that. Reach and point the rod down while he's in the air. *You* don't do the bowing, you bow the tip of the rod down."

Fortunately, the tarpon gave me another chance to redeem myself and my bowing technique.

It continued to pull and strain, begging to yank me overboard. I spoke to my captain in a strange and nervous voice, with the same insecurity I had felt after seventeen hours of labor contractions finally consumed me and my courage, and

I began to crack. I asked my captain the same question I had asked my nurse: "Am I doing this right?"

"Just keep pressure on him."

To get enough leverage I had to push the fighting butt of the rod into my stomach. Because of the pain, I moved it every five minutes to a new spot. I tattooed myself with the rod butt. Later the spots turned purple. I felt proud. Battle scars to remind me that the tarpon had been determined to continue on its migratory run through the Keys, with or without me.

"Aren't we going to follow him?" I asked as the tarpon slipped farther and farther away.

"No. If we follow him, we will only be giving him a rest. Keep the pressure on."

Straining and pulling, I tried to force the rod tip up and wrestle my tarpon to the surface. I felt like I might as well be trying to lift the corner of a house.

"When he goes right, you go left."

My guide was more relaxed than he had been earlier. I understood him. He had done his part by getting me into a fish; now it was my turn to go to work. From this point on, his day was officially over. Unless he blew the gaff or release, he had done his job. If I made a mistake and lost this battle, "Well," he could say, "she had her chance."

He stood next to me and chewed on a cigar. Our catch had not gone unnoticed by the boats lined up to our right. We both felt a little smug about that.

"How long will it take?" I asked.

"Oh, I'd say you have about an hour or more to go."

The same response the nurse had given me when I asked how long I would have to push before my baby was born; the same feelings of dread and determination followed.

Interesting how intimacy with strangers develops. Modesty is abandoned on the delivery room table when the nurse reaches in to check your cervix as if checking a roast, and says things like, "Don't worry about that bowel movement, it happens all the time." Your captain, guiding you to a runaway athlete of the ocean, stands by glibly as you torque yourself into strange, half-crouched positions and make grunting sounds you did not even know you could. In both cases you give yourself over. Nurse or captain, they become your guardian. You depend on them. In a way you become their child, venturing a short distance ahead as you tangle with the forces of nature.

Bits of chewed tobacco had dried in the corners of his mouth and on his chin. "You want a Coke?" he asked.

"Ah, maybe a little later," I answered, wondering how I was supposed to drink and fight at the same time. I moved the rod butt up on my hip.

"This is like an arm-wrestling match," I commented. "We're just pushing and pulling and nothing is happening."

After a half-hour, I felt something lighten at the end of the line. Inch by inch I could reel in. It was another half-hour before my guide stretched out over the bow on his belly and reached for the leader. We had agreed earlier that all fish would be released. He grabbed and jerked the leader so that it broke.

Relief. Blood rushed back into my shoulders. My legs quaked with exhaustion. I felt dizzy and weightless. The line blew freely in the breeze as my born-again tarpon child swam away. My captain stood up and gave me a congratulatory hug and handshake. It was late in the afternoon. He pulled up the stake and started the engine. I felt a little displaced.

The skiff jammed home over ocean waves. The wind became a G force, distorting the face, flattening the lips. Freedom and power come with speed. The victorious come flying home on the wings of salt water. Somewhere out in the Atlantic, a leader trailed behind a tarpon like an umbilical cord as it searched its way through the sea back to its tribe.

I had caught a tarpon. A ninety-five-pound tarpon. I could sit at Papa Joe's bar afterward, and when someone asked, "How'd you do today?" I would not have to find words to veil disappointment.

The Gold Cup participants met back at Papa Joe's to record their catches on easels draped with broad white sheets of paper. Scores for teams and individuals were squeaked onto the paper with thick, colored markers by a woman in a bikini top and shorts.

Women who had waited all day on land arrived fresh from their showers, their painted toenails peeking out from expensive leather sandals. With sunglasses pushed up on top of their heads, they held drinks and posed next to their men. Guides teased and bragged. Fishermen who smelled of sweat and sunscreen leaned across the varnished tables to talk. There was laughter and stories, and some guarded and not-so-guarded disappointments.

Four days were left in the tournament. A few of those who had bragged too much before the Gold Cup felt humiliated by their score of zero. Some, who had kept quiet, calculated that their releases put them ahead, with a chance to place. "It's not over till it's over," someone postulated above the din of the crowd.

I sat quietly with my captain, reviewing our day, watching the people around us, and enjoying the way the salt on the rim of the glass blended into my margarita with each sip, when someone grabbed my arm and lifted me up off the bar stool. Immediately I pulled back and reached to pry his fingers away. He was one of the tournament participants and his red face lunged toward mine and sneered, "Wasn't it you who cut in front of me today?"

"What are you talking about," I stammered, still trying to pull away from his grip.

My captain rose up off his stool and shouted at my assailant, "I wasn't any where near your goddamn boat."

"I thought I saw you cut in front of me."

"Where?" my captain asked. Mr. Manners continued to hold my arm, dangling me in midair above my seat. He named a place six miles north of where we had been staked.

"We weren't anywhere near you," my captain snorted.

My accuser let go, leaving red marks where his fingers had been. I dropped back onto the bar stool and rubbed my arm, trying to make the feel of his hand and the marks disappear.

"Jesus Christ! What the hell's the matter with him?" my captain said as he studied the man's retreat across the room.

You gotta love the Keys.

I watched anglers try to bribe. A thin man with a gold bracelet offered my captain double his fee if he would come out of retirement to fish the Gold Cup the next year.

"No, I don't fish tournaments any more, thanks anyway."

Later, another man pushed through the crowd and offered him more money than the first.

"No, I don't fish tournaments any more."

He meant what he said.

The noise in the bar dropped as anglers drifted out. I left to join friends for dinner. My captain followed me out the door. I wanted to tell him that in connecting with the tarpon I had felt transformed yet at the same time like a tourist who, for a precious few moments, had dropped into the bright, living waters off Islamorada for a glimpse of something real, and powerful, and wild—then was prematurely escorted home. I had been given a taste of the ocean wilderness and I wanted to go back, not just because I wanted to count tarpon coups, but because I wanted to listen to the water. To see what dream would float by next and to wish for it to grab my fly and drag me, body and soul, after it.

My captain, who had been called to Keys waters for over twenty years, must have heard what I was thinking. He winked as we parted.

"Be ready at five-thirty again tomorrow, and we'll go fishin'."

Granddad

I was stalling. Holding a coffee cup with only cold coffee left at the bottom, I stood in the rain outside the tackle shop conversing with another outfitter. Everyone else, including my clients, was inside the shop, looking comfortable in the warm glow of light that burned in the windows and defied the dark, rainy weather outside.

Hands in pockets, shoulders hunched, mustache dripping with water, my guide friend gave me a spring creek update.

"This will be a great day for *Baetis*. They started coming off yesterday, but the weather is worse today and the hatch should be fantastic. Do you have any in sizes 20 or 22? Good. You'll need about a half-dozen of each."

He kept apologizing for sounding like he was telling me what to do, and I kept reassuring him that I did not mind that he wanted to tell me what to do. I did not mind because it made me look like I had important business standing in the rain, which I actually had, since I had not been on the spring creek for several weeks and needed a boost of information. I needed a morale boost as well. I was tired. The guide season had begun in May and was coming too slowly to an end. It was September, and I still had over two weeks to go before my wading boots would have a chance to dry.

I kept my eye on the shop's door, thinking, "Just five more minutes, I want five more minutes."

But the door burst open before my grace period was up, and two gentlemen clients walked out as if they owned the day.

"Here they come," my friend warned quietly.

Recognizing me huddled by my Jeep, they marched over with outstretched arms and proceeded to shake my hand with the enthusiasm of long-lost friends. The cold coffee sloshed around in my cup.

I peered out from under my soggy cowboy hat and saw the friendly faces of two brothers at the beginning of their Montana fishing trip. They were not bossy, puffed-up executive types, or suspicious professor types either.

"It's so good to meet you!" they both exclaimed.

They were genuine. I relaxed. I led them back into the tackle shop to pick out a few flies.

*7*he Jeep bounced over the cattle guard at the front entrance to the spring creek property and followed the dirt road to the main house, where we would pay our rod fees. It was as if my passengers, Gary and Vann, were on a trip to Disneyland.

"Gosh, isn't this just great, Vann? We finally made it. I never thought we would make it!"

"You wouldn't believe how excited we are to be. . . . Hey! Stop the car. Look, Gary, that's where we saw Jennifer on TV!"

I could feel myself blush.

"That's where she was fishing with Larry," Gary said as he turned toward me. "I remember the part where you netted a big rainbow right over there."

I had been featured on a show called *Fishing the West*, and apparently both men had seen the program. I wanted to change the subject.

"Can we fish back there where you were on TV?" asked Gary.

"Sure. Sure, if you want to. We could start there and later on I could show you other parts of the creek," I said.

"Great. This is really a dream come true," Gary said.

It was so easy. I felt like I had served everyone a Happy Meal. I could have kicked myself for being so apprehensive that morning.

We put on our gear and strung our rods. I positioned the brothers on the creek and worked with each one. Two brothers from Staunton, Virginia. I felt I had joined them in the living room of their childhood home. A place where, even with an eleven-year age difference, they had been close. At one point, Gary, who had booked me more than six months ahead, took me aside, put a hand on my shoulder, and said, "My brother loves to fish. There isn't anything I'd like to see more than for him to catch a fish with you today."

Later, Vann took me aside, put a hand on my shoulder, and said, "Jennifer, Gary paid for this trip and everything. I'm just happy to be here. Don't spend too much time with me. I want him to catch a fish."

I wanted to float above them with a magic fish wand and make fish appear all around. Instead, I had to remain on earth armed with only my fly rod and my shouted instructions.

"Mend. Mend again. Pick it up. Take two steps. Cast again." I breathed down their necks as they followed my advice.

Vann finally got into a fish that acted like a hen being chased by a fox. It ran back and forth in front of us, then fled for its life downstream, where it surged into warp speed and broke free. Not a feather was left. A new fly and tippet were tied on.

Gary was less experienced than his brother, but no less enthusiastic. He listened politely to my lessons on nymphing and immediately went to work while I studied and offered thumbs-up and thumbs-down reviews of his presentations.

Like chess pieces, I moved the brothers around the creek—backward, forward, and sideways—trying to position them over a rising trout, or put them near a lie where a nymphing trout was feeding. The much-discussed *Baetis* hatch was stunted due to improved weather conditions, and the trout were as tired as the guides who had fished over them for the past five months. Lunch became the obvious solution to a slow morning.

I whistled in Vann and Gary after setting the picnic table with a simple lunch of soup and sandwiches, fruit, and chocolate chip cookies. They acted as if I had just served them Thanksgiving dinner.

In a soft Virginia voice that had a hint of a southern accent, Vann said, "I know someone who would love to be here right now."

"I think he is here," replied Gary.

"Feels like it, doesn't it?" said Vann.

"Who?" I asked.

"Granddad," they both answered.

Their granddad, Elmer Knighting, was their hero. He was the one who took them fishing every Saturday. He was the gentle, thoughtful one who packed Dr Peppers and sandwiches for lunch and forsook all other duties for the company of his grandchildren, who wanted to follow him in the fine art of angling with a worm. He shared his tele-scoping aluminum poles, Sears fiberglass rods, nets, tackle box, and worming equipment with them, and from those days emerged enough pleasant memories to carry the brothers through a lifetime.

Granddad was the adult you could depend on. He lived across the street and left the door open. It always seemed that he loomed larger than life in their lives. Gary remarked that it was only after Granddad died that he real-ized the man was only five-foot-eight and weighed about a hundred fifty pounds. "I always thought he was bigger than that."

Now, when fishing by himself, Gary confessed he felt a confidence, and a lack of loneliness; a feeling that his grandfather was there. I was glad to know that such a grandfather had actually inhabited the earth, and did not just exist in ads for Wertners candies.

"I would like to make a toast." Gary placed a bottle of Blanton's single-barrel bourbon in front of us. It was an unusual bottle, sculpted like a barrel and topped with a cork that had been adorned with a bronze jockey rid-ing his thoroughbred at top speed. Perhaps an allusion to how you might feel upon tasting the special-edition con-tents of the bottle. We held out empty coffee cups to receive a splash.

"This is something I've been working for this very moment," said Gary with a sudden shyness. A silence, like the kind when families bow heads to pray before a meal, followed. Gary made his toast:

Here's to the fishers and here's to the flies
The dry, and the nymph, and the wet
And here's to the Old Man, the Guide,
   and the River
And here's to the trout in the net.

We raised our cups, nodded to each other, and drank. Round, rich, and woody, the bourbon warmed my mouth and came alive with the flavor and scent of cedar. It trickled down the back of my throat, leaving me a little surprised with the need for air.

The brothers became quiet and contemplative. I thought I detected a tear in Gary's eyes. Suddenly I was in the center of a triangle of Vann, Gary, and Granddad. The moment had a distilled quality, and all that was needed was to let it be.

On the creek again, we waited for *Baetis*. One or two floated by, giving us the impression that more would be on the way. Trout began to make themselves known by dimpling the surface with noses and dorsal fins. Like raindrops, here and there, they began to rise. The water's surface became agitated with life.

"Breathe easy," I thought, "the hard part's over. Watch while Mother Nature takes care of these gentlemen from Virginia."

But as the hour progressed without a hookup, my dream of netting fish after fish turned into a guide's nightmare.

"You can see 'em, but you can't catch 'em," said Vann playfully. "It's enough to make a grown man cry."

"And a guide," I added.

Dancing the two-step back and forth between Vann and Gary, I altered nymph leaders, changing length, changing tippets. I augmented leaders with lead, took it off, put it back on again. I raced through fly boxes, staring and studying patterns, talking to the flies, asking them, "Which one of you guys do they want?" The boxes remained mute. The sound of sipping trout, like dripping faucets, continued.

Where were my powers? Where was that smiling guide on the front of the brochure full of promises to improve your knowledge of fly casting and fly fishing?

"Call the Better Business Bureau, call the police, we have a thief, a fraud," I thought.

My wading boots felt heavy.

In frustration I stood on the bank and tried to figure out how to trick my way into the head of a trout. That is when I noticed the way the trout were feeding. Slurp-slurp-slurp, in short, quick nips at the surface. Midging. They were midging. I opened my fly box and the Griffith Gnats piled up by the tens and twenties seemed to shout, "We were here all along!"

One Griffith Gnat on a twelve-foot 7X tippet later, Gary brought a bright, lively rainbow to my net. Whoops and whistles drowned out the peace and quiet that had prevailed on the river all day. We were obnoxious with joy. If I ever find out what drug works for guide anxiety, I am going to take it. Until then, the best cure is a client with a fish. Arms around each other, Gary and I posed for the camera. Flash. Click. Whurr. Another trophy day. I could pin my guide badge back on.

Waving good-bye to the Knighting brothers, I felt the kind of nostalgia you feel after a holiday spent with relatives that, for the first time in years, went surprisingly well. You need to go home, but you do not want to. You cannot believe that, for once, nobody was insulted, became jealous, felt put upon or put out. Nobody's covered dish was left uneaten. Nobody wanted to take his gift back and have it exchanged for something he liked better. Everyone left satisfied.

Also as at Christmas, I departed with a bagful of gifts. I had protested, saying, "No, no, you shouldn't do that," but I drove away with the rest of the Blanton's bourbon, a mosaic hat pin in the shape of a fish that I had admired on Gary's hat, and six size 14 Granddad flies designed and tied by Vann.

The Granddad flies had divided wings of bright orange. Mixed brown and grizzly hackles, wound tightly next to a plump, peacock herl body, that bumped up next to an elk hair tail.

"I designed these flies after fishing with Granddad," Vann said. "They remind me of the days I spent with him and of all the brook trout I used to catch on Ramsey's Draft. Granddad would always stop to admire the brook trout, saying, 'Isn't it pretty,' before letting it go. I've sure caught a lot of brookies with this fly."

"I've never seen you do that before," joked Gary. "You never give flies to anyone."

A week later, I was guiding a woman on the Gallatin River and feeling down because it was late in the day and we had not caught anything.

"Why don't you go ahead and fish," she offered.

I tied on a Granddad fly just to see how it would do. First cast, second cast, then *snap!* A fish sucked it under. I reeled it in. It was a brook trout.

"Wow," I said to myself.

Wow. I had never caught a brook trout in the Gallatin before.

I did not know what to make of it. Was it Granddad winking at me from the heavens? Or was it a bread crumb to remind me I was on the right track? The brookie's bright spots of orange circled in blue like small targets glowed on its soft, slippery skin. I heard myself say, "Thanks, Granddad." Thanks for the fish and thanks for the mystery.

When I am trying to catch fish for clients and that guide anxiety starts to creep in, because I cannot get their flies to land where fish will bite, I think of Granddad, a man who loved kids, Saturdays, and Dr Pepper. A man who taught that there are more important things than catching fish, and there are less important things than catching fish, and we are not alone.

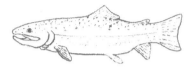

We've Seen the Movie

"*I* know we didn't talk about this before, but my thirteen-year-old daughter is coming along, too. We hope you don't mind," said the mother.

Instead of two, I would have three to guide the next morning.

Having a chance to make an impression on a thirteen-year-old girl might be fun, I mused. Thirteen was the age I was when my father took me fly fishing for the first time. I suddenly felt excited about the possibilities for this introduction to rivers and trout. "I hope she likes me," I wished aloud.

The next day was bright and windless. Across the valley, the Bridger Mountains shone dark and strong and powerful in the morning light. "This will be a great day," I announced.

My clients were waiting for me in front of the guest house where they were staying. The mother, Penny, was petite; the stepfather, Riley, smiling. The daughter, Amy, stood with arms folded across her chest. Rental rods and gear were circulated and the casting lessons began.

It was a usual mix of talents. The stepfather was patient and persistent. The mother would make one or two great casts, then ten that she would critique by saying, "that wasn't it, that wasn't it. What am I doing wrong?" Amy chewed gum and excused herself several times to eat from a bag of potato chips.

The mother became distracted by her daughter's lack of interest. "Amy, now come out here and try to do this," she requested. As I worked with her stepfather, who continued to practice and improve, the teenager slowly crossed the lawn and picked up the rod I had set up for her.

"Good, Riley! Much better," I was saying. "Don't drop the rod tip so low in the front on the second stop. Keep the tip up and let the line straighten out in front of you before you lower the rod tip."

"You can't do it, Riley!" Amy interrupted. "You're too uncoordinated."

Riley maintained his composure and said nothing.

"Did you hear me, Riley?"

"Yeah, I heard you, honey."

"Jennifer, look at me. What do you think of me?" Amy demanded.

"I think you need more practice," I said. I went to reorganize her casting stroke.

"Oh, Amy, you're doing a wonderful job," said the mother. "Isn't she, Riley?"

Deep in concentration, Riley nodded and responded, "Yeah, ah um."

"Riley! Look at her! You're not looking," said the mother.

Graciously, Riley stopped casting and watched while I coached Amy. Her stroke began to improve.

"Better, Amy," I commented.

"I'm going to beat you, Riley," she said.

The morning started to deteriorate around eleven. Riley continued to improve; the women, distracted and bored, laid down their rods. "When's lunch? When are we leaving?" whined Amy. I set the table for lunch on the porch of the guest house.

"It's hot here. Something smells," said Amy.

"They just oiled the wooden porch," I explained.

"It's disgusting," she said.

After lunch we loaded fly rods and fishing gear into the cars and started the drive to the Gallatin Canyon. Amy made a point of riding with me. I mistakenly took this as a good sign.

"I have a boyfriend. My mother hates him," my passenger blurted out after five miles.

"Why?"

"He's eighteen."

She continued. "My mother, she always tells me to get off the phone because she doesn't want me talking to him. So once when I was talking late at night, I told her I wouldn't get off the phone until I was ready. She didn't do anything. She never does. Riley, he's afraid of me."

"Have you ever gone fishing before?" I asked, trying to change the subject.

"No, but we've seen the movie *A River Runs Through It.*" The waters of the Gallatin sparkled. I crossed a bridge that would take us upstream along the east side, on a bumpy dirt road. It is a moody river. During spring runoff, snows from the Gallatin Range dissolve into droplets and become swollen streams that tumble down crevices and valleys and end up raging in one muddy voice down the canyon, racing for the Missouri. The Gallatin has taken the lives of kayakers, inner-tube riders, and anglers; drivers have lost control of their cars and plunged into her rushing waters. But that day, the Gallatin was calm and full of life. She was ready to receive visitors and permit them to play in her currents.

I pulled off the main road and opened the car door in the settling dust. Amy's parents parked behind me and huddled near my tailgate while I organized the tackle.

"Have you ever seen a bear?" the mother asked.

"I've seen several along the Gallatin this summer. I've never seen any up here, though."

"Ever seen a grizzly?"

"Not up here."

I tried to sound casual as I uncapped rod cases and handed out wading gear.

"If we meet a bear, which we won't, the most important thing to try to do is to stay calm. Back away slowly, and try to get away quietly. If you have the misfortune of being attacked, curl up in a ball and try to keep your face and neck protected with your arms. I carry pepper spray with me, so I'll do my best to get the bear away. We all need to keep our ears and eyes open, it's part of being in the woods, but don't worry too much about it. I haven't run into any bears on guiding trips."

"I have to pee," said the daughter.

"You can go down the hill there in the bushes," I answered.

I turned to unload more gear from the back of the Jeep.

"Pee out here? No way! I am not going to pee out here. I have to have an outhouse," she protested.

"The outhouse is two miles up the road," I said.

"Good, you can take me there," she said as she parked herself in my front seat and slammed the door.

"Me too," said the mother. "I have to pee, too."

I looked at Riley for sympathy. He shrugged his shoulders. It looked like a habit.

The campground near the outhouses was the site of a college frat party. Rock and roll boomed from boom boxes, Frisbees were flying, kegs of beer were being tapped, and trucks filled with college coeds were pulling in by twos and threes. A thin German shepherd wearing a red bandanna walked by. I felt awkward in my waders and cowboy hat. The mother looked alarmed, the daughter delighted.

After visiting the outhouse, we drove back to where Riley patiently waited for us. I was finally able to herd all three of them, dressed and ready to fish, down to the river's edge.

"Riley, you work this riffle from this boulder up to the fallen tree. I'll move Amy upstream from you, and I'll take Penny upstream from Amy. I'll rotate between the three of you, so you'll see me in a few minutes. Holler if you catch one."

Riley was eager and ready to go. You can tell when a person has the fishing spirit. I watched as he let himself become absorbed by the river. I could see that a boyish part of him had returned as he stood with innocent curiosity, rod in hand, making the fly drift in short, accurate floats. I knew he would catch a fish, and he did. It was his first fish on a fly rod.

Everyone gathered by the bank as I lifted up his brook trout for him to admire.

"Honey, go up and get the camera," he asked.

"Oh Riley, it's just a little fish," said Amy.

"I don't want to go all the way back to the car," said Penny.

"I'll get the camera," I offered.

"Just put it back, Riley," said Penny, and she walked away.

Riley shrugged, "I guess we should just put it back."

I sighed in disgust.

Amy decided she would rather wade in the creek and throw rocks than fish. I put her in a place where she could have that freedom.

Her mother reluctantly followed me upstream. Around a curve in the river and out of sight of her daughter, Penny became agitated.

"I don't trust her," she blurted. "I never know what she's going to do next. She's my only child. I know I'm overprotective, but—could you go see what she's doing?"

"She's just around the corner exploring the river. She won't go anywhere."

"You don't know her."

Penny shifted from one foot to the other.

"Back home I make her wear a beeper. When I page her, she has to call me right away."

Clearly, I was no longer a fishing guide, I was a part of the family dynamic. The trip and my professionalism were being sabotaged by people who could not take anything but themselves seriously. I had a job to do. The person who wanted to be guided was Riley. The attention that Riley should have been getting was being taken away by the women in his family. I decided that my duty was to take care of Riley and let the women follow as best they could.

The daughter was casting rocks and wading knee-deep in the water where I had left her. I felt that this immersion in nature was good for her and did not mind that her interest in fishing had disappeared. Her nervous mother, who had yet to put a fly on the water, followed me and decided to stay and watch her daughter throw stones.

"I'm going to work with Riley for a while."

"How long are you going to be gone?" asked Penny.

"About ten minutes or so."

Riley and I left long faces and a deep silence behind. The farther we got from the women, the more insecure he became.

"I think we're going to have to go pretty soon," he said.

"You mean, leave for Bozeman?"

"Yeah, the girls are getting tired."

I took him to a deep, green pool upstream and around the corner from his family. Trout were rising. Riley and I began to get lost in our fishing. I showed him the golden stone fly that the fish were taking; we discussed which pattern he should tie on to imitate it. Wearing my guide's hat straight for the first time that day, I took delight in talking him through the presentation. Our communication grew and the distractions from the others were gradually forgotten. We had begun to enter the fly fisher's world of trying to connect with nature when the day came to a crashing end.

Screams, shrill and hysterical, sounded through the pines. Instinctively, I grabbed the canister of pepper spray from its strap on my hip and pulled off the safety cap. Charging through the thick brush and willows, I blindly followed the sounds of people in trouble. "Bear, moose, or snake," I concluded. Jumping off the bank and into the current, I arrived with a splash to find Penny standing in the river, hands cupped around her mouth, yelling her husband's name. Amy was on the bank in the same position.

No animals. No blood.

"What's the matter?" I demanded.

"Riley's ten minutes are up. We want to go," retorted Penny.

She stepped out of the river with arms folded across her chest and in a chilly silence faced her daughter. I turned and saw Riley coming through the trees, spooling his line.

"I guess we better go," he said quietly.

I walked to my car swimming with fury.

Down the hill from where the cars were parked, I could hear Penny and Amy arguing. They grew louder, but I could only hear fragments of what they were saying.

"Shut up!"

"No, you shut up!"

Riley shuffled by me as I pulled a soda out of my cooler.

"They're arguing about where they should pee," said Riley as he removed his waders and began to put his gear away.

"Jennifer," he continued calmly, "do you know of a restaurant in town that serves alcohol?"

"I'll make you a list," I said.

I had two hours left before I had to be home. As soon as Riley, Penny, and Amy were down the road I decided I would return to the dark, green pool with the rising trout, stand next to it in the sunshine, and dance a dry fly on its surface.

Just before they drove off, Amy noticed that I was still in waders and had strung my fly rod. She stuck her head out the car window as Riley pulled away.

"What are you doing?"

"I'm going fishing."

"You're crazy!" she shouted as she made a face.

Dust from their car blew over me. I turned and headed for the river.

Motherless Daughter: Add Water

*M*y father baptized me as a fly fisher in the waters of the Madison River. My mother had died from breast cancer a month earlier. I was thirteen. A handful of flies were dropped into my palm and instructions were pointed out by the tip of a fly rod.

"Fish that area over there in front of the rock and behind the rock. Fish against that bank. Fish between the quiet water and the fast water. I'll be back."

This was our vacation. I was there to begin again. I was there to let the picture of my mother's hospital room and the last time I saw her sink beneath the surface and float away.

I listened to the sound of his waders as he walked upstream. I stepped into the Madison of late June in tennis shoes and jeans. Skinny. Cold. Determined. The sun warmed my shoulders and back. I was surrounded by green fields, protected by mountains on the horizon. The sweet smell of willows, like incense, drifted on the breeze. I felt safe.

They say people fight a brave battle with cancer. My mother barely had a chance to raise her sword. The cancer went into remission, but then it marched a final campaign into her lymph nodes, spine, and stomach. The doctors tried to save her by making a hasty retreat. They removed her breasts, ovaries, and uterus. "They took everything away from me," she said to her sister, then despite everyone's efforts the cancer took the rest.

The last time I saw my mother in the hospital I did not know that I had come to say good-bye. I thought I was being allowed to say hello after being kept away week after week. She never said good-bye. She did not leave a note or a message. No word from her telling me she thought she would be leaving. One morning she was gone and her silence only deepened.

When I look back upon my childhood searching for her face beneath the reflective surface of memory, I catch a rare glimpse. The clothes she wore, her dark hair. The way we drove to the grocery store, me asking question after question until her answer became an exasperated, "I don't know. I don't know how the gills get the oxygen from the water, they just do."

Staring into the river I could not see any fish. The nuns told me after her funeral, "You can't see her, but she is there." I cast.

The water was so cold my teeth chattered. I got tangled for the tenth time. The leader became wrapped and knotted around willow branches. I carefully removed it without damaging it or breaking off the fly. The leader finally loose, I felt satisfied. Something had worked out.

A Royal Wulff rode the current. I was reminded of puppet shows where the pull of a string made arms and legs move. I pulled the string up and my fly flew. Back on the water again. Up. Back on the water again. Up. Over the water. Down. It was fun just trying. Suddenly it went under. I wanted it back! I pulled and my line vibrated with life. I screamed because it felt so odd. I pulled. It pulled back. I screamed again. I wanted to see it.

My father heard me scream and came ready with the net. He scooped up my rainbow. We were both excited. Naturally, since he is a lawyer, he asked a lot of questions. "Where did you catch it? Did you see it strike? How many strikes did you have before you caught it?"

That was the beginning of my afterlife. I cast again. I wanted to see what else was there. I needed to know.

"Are you there? Are you there?" my fly called.

I have had this communication with water ever since. Rivers have become my consolation. Places where I go to practice asking questions. The fish seem to listen. I pull up fish after fish as if I am looking for something. Each one is a pleasure and a disappointment at the same time.

Like a spoiled person, I put them back and look for more. I never seem satisfied, and yet, the plucking of fish from rivers and oceans satisfies me. I feel that I am solving a mystery. My mystery.

Sometimes I try to reach into the past, the one where my mother existed, and understand who she was, so I might know who I am.

"You were too young to know her," I was told.

I was told that she wanted to protect us, my brother and me, by not telling us about her cancer.

"She didn't want to frighten you. She wanted to live," people said.

"She was in denial," I decided after a year of counseling.

I stand in rivers and try to see what lies beneath the surface. My whole life feels like a quest to see what is under the surface. Having been tricked by secrets before, I look into people's faces, and when their words form I try to see what they are really saying. I will not be fooled again.

I play tricks myself. My fly is an illusion. The trout want it, thinking it is something to eat, something that will sustain them; so they take it, and try to swim back unnoticed to the comfort of their rocks. But they soon discover that it is me.

I do not keep fish. I want our relationship to go on and on. I like to come back to the banks of my summers and cast into rivers of past and present, in places like Three Dollar Bridge on the Madison. My father and I always caught fish there. It was a favorite place for us. I followed him like a shadow. He fished ahead of me, moving in and out of the current, looking for the perfect spot to drop his fly. He did not talk a lot about fishing, he just did it. He was always happy to catch fish, but it never ruined his day to not catch fish.

He never took care of his tackle. Rods were tossed willy-nilly into the back of the station wagon, wet fly boxes were left shut. I learned early that *to fish* was the most important act. Everything surrounding it, including lunch, was incidental. My cerebral father fished like he read books: voraciously and with great concentration. I imitated his style. It kept my mind off other things. Replacing other things with the movement of water and surges of life at the end of the line became the reason to go fishing. I began to heal.

But water cannot be completely trusted. Once, I stepped into the Snake River during the end of spring runoff. I saw where I thought a fish should be and started to wade toward it. I was pushed and shoved downstream as if I had been caught in a rush for the stage at a rock concert. I lost my footing and was carried away. At fifteen I never thought I could get hurt. I just thought I had been clumsy and would be in quiet water soon. I had never been in trouble with water before.

A boulder that had collected a log-and-brush snag stopped my tumbling, wet ride. I pulled myself up and noticed that my father had quit fishing and tracked me anxiously downstream. He paced the bank looking for the best way to wade out and retrieve me. We struggled out of the river together. He broke the current above me with his body and held me tight by the arm. Back at the car, I fit myself into an oversized shirt and pants that had been left in the backseat, while my father recovered by reviewing my wading mistake, demanding that I be more careful in the future.

I had such faith in water. I had much to learn.

It is Breast Cancer Awareness Week at Bozeman Deaconess Hospital. Today, I am a careful adult woman. I make an appointment. I am given a flyer with a diagram showing how to feel for lumps. "Breast cancer may be cured if you find it early. Check your breasts about one week after your period by moving your fingers in a circular motion like this. . . ." The picture makes the breasts look like targets with nipples as bull's-eyes. "If your mother or sister has had breast cancer you are in the high risk group. You have a greater chance than other women of getting breast cancer. Be sure to check your breasts regularly and tell your doctor right away if you find any lumps, knots, or changes." It will not happen to me. I tell myself that I am different. I live a healthy life. I will not get cancer. Only denial runs in my family.

Mammogram. The cold machine presses my breasts into pyramid pancakes. She did not have this machine. My guilt grows and my anger grows, and I am sorry to be angry, and I am angry that I feel sorry. My tears drip onto the machine.

"Does it hurt?" the technician asks.

I piece together her life by the photographs and scrapbooks that were left on a shelf for me to find. She lives in her baby pictures. She lives in the professional photos taken of her and her horse when she showed her American Saddle Bred as a teenager. Her high school graduation portrait, and the photo of her with her sorority sisters at UCLA, show a beauty with dark, straight hair and high cheekbones. She appears in a page in *Mademoiselle* magazine as a model. Yellowed newspaper clippings of her engagement and wedding announcements almost tear as my hands turn the page. She embraces my brother and me for the camera on the front porch of our home. I cradle those dusty books in my arms. The woman between the pages should be someone I know, but she is not. Time has stolen the sound of her voice from me.

It is on rivers that I try to make the fragments of memory whole, and the meaning clear. It is to water that I go to be alone, to ask the whys of life, to pull up fish like answers knowing I will never find them all.

Hooks & Barbs

*I*t had all the ingredients for a great day. A good trout stream, a box full of flies, a section of river all to myself, and my dad as a fishing companion. Yet with every fish he hauled in I grew more and more incompetent and strange. My fly rod did not seem to be mine anymore. The knots in my leader had became a metaphor for the day.

I realized that I had focused on a particular piece of water for over two hours and caught only willows and sagebrush, while my father's flies had flown tangle-free, and his fly rod, in the ethereal light of a Madison River evening, had bowed to the weight of a trout every twenty minutes.

Overwhelmed by frustration, I had to know what he was doing that I was not. Life itself seemed upstream as I waded toward my father, pushing through the current that threatened to topple me. I stood next to him, hoping he would see how I could not tolerate any further humiliation.

"I haven't caught anything."

"I noticed you haven't. What the hell have you been doing? They're all over the place. They're taking a Royal Trude. I'll show you where to cast and you'll get one."

The tired, insane person who lives in me started to argue with the stubborn, but sane, person who also lives in me. They rose up from their respective tables and started a mental barroom brawl. Chairs and bottles were flung. Punches were landed. The insane person held the sane person down and responded to my dear father, who was landing yet another fish, "I don't need you or anyone else to tell me how to catch a fish. I'll do it myself."

And I stomped off to the top of the island, uttering words that made my father wince.

My father's fly landed softly and delicately right on the spot he had offered to me moments before, and caught another trout.

"See, I told you there was a fish there!"

For more than an hour I could not look at him. I did not catch any fish that evening either.

Why do we fall apart on rivers? Mental scales, measuring tapes, and calculators come popping out of vest pockets that should be zippered shut and locked. Other people's good luck suddenly becomes your own bad luck. As they grow, you shrink, until you feel like nobody, and begin to believe that the trout, with a brain the size of a pea, laughs.

*W*e hire guides like lawyers, believing they will get us the settlement we want, trusting they will do the job for us—we dare not fail too much on our own. We tip guides if we feel good about ourselves and the day. We grow silent and tight with guides when our lack of skill or luck becomes too obvious.

I once guided a gentleman on a well-known spring creek near Livingston, Montana. He had been in a good humor most of the day, but as the hours ticked by his optimism began to bleach out with the intensity of the sun.

The day was bright and breezy, and the fish were extra-spooky. None would sip, kiss, or even sniff his dry fly. His equipment was too heavy for the quiet surface of the spring creek. I offered him my Scott 4-weight, but he insisted on his 6-weight. I demonstrated how to delicately pick up line from the surface, and encouraged him to lay down the line gently. I remained calm while a spray of water misted the air when he yanked up the rod tip and asked, "How's that?"

There had been a brilliant opportunity to float a downstream drift to a massive and cautious brown, but patience and skill would not hold hands, and after two casts, the brown left for a quieter neighborhood.

"Let's change this fly. I don't think this fly is working," he demanded, while his dragging fly made little wakes in the water.

I could see large, healthy trout feeding on emergers. My client insisted that they were taking adults and I was unable to convince him otherwise. I begged him to keep as much of his fly line off the water as possible by keeping the rod tip high. He began to improve until mysterious clumps of grassy vegetation started to float by. It looked like someone had mowed the field upstream and dumped the clippings in. Just as my client's fly settled in for a foot-long-drag-free float, a clump of grass caught up with it and ran it over. He brought in his fly, pulled the grass off the hook, and cast again. In less than a minute a strand of grass snagged his newly presented fly. Then all casual chatter ceased. I offered directions and made suggestions, but he had quit talking. Trout rose and bumped the surface up and down the creek. Grass ran over his fly every other cast.

I felt it coming. I should have moved him sooner. He finally took a reading on his Failure Odometer and burst out shouting, "This is nothing but a goddamn whorehouse! I want my money back. I can't fish in this shit. Look at this. Why do I have to pay to fish in this shit?"

"Let's move downstream, the grass isn't as bad down there," I said.

My client quizzed fly fishers and guides all the way down the stream, asking them what they thought of the grass floating around in the creek and if they had caught anything.

This is always a tricky thing to do: to expose yourself. People may console you through commiseration, but you run the risk of discovering that you are, indeed, a loser. Fortunately, fly fishers have developed a wonderful face-saving language to explain fishlessness. If someone should ask, "How's the fishing," and you have not caught anything, you can say, "It's been slow." You might want to add, ". . . but interesting." This allows the conversation to drift toward a discussion of the insect life, a few notable rises against the bank, and the weather. You are allowed to have your dignity, your privacy, and your fishlessness without having to go into details.

My desperate client's fishless day was crawling all over him. Anglers he spoke to gave him a wry smile and said, "It's been slow, but good." The translation being that, despite the difficult conditions, a fish had been caught. My client became more withdrawn and began working the muscles in his jaw. One of my guide friends winked at me as we walked past. I rolled my eyes skyward.

There were better opportunities to present a fly at our new location. A woman upstream from us who had been standing in the same spot almost all day squealed as she cranked in a beautiful rainbow trout.

"This has just been a marvelous day." We overheard her praise her guide as she spooled her line. Praise I knew I was not going to hear from my client. Their satisfaction bloomed like roses. Handshakes, and slaps on the back, and cheerful banter echoed as they returned to their vehicle. My client saw his chances dwindle like the light of a setting sun. I could already feel the awkwardness of accepting his check.

I tied on a fresh tippet, greased his leader, and insisted that he cast the pheasant tail nymph upstream. He managed to catch a decent rainbow. My shoulders sank with relief. My smile returned. But for him, it was too little, too late.

"I'm not kidding. I think that paying a rod fee to fish this creek with all this junk in the water is wrong. I think you should talk to somebody about it. I'll never come here again," he declared.

Distance between loved ones and loved rivers grows quickly when people's expectations of the fishing and of themselves are not met. These strange moments seem to come from nowhere, and once they begin, they seem to take on a life of their own. Succumbing to jealousy, anxiety, or anger when fishing is something no one is proud of. But it happens to everyone. It is usually only slightly less difficult to witness someone else's moment of despair than your own although, occasionally, it can be oddly satisfying.

For instance, my older brother and I have a complicated, competitive relationship. Once, in a weak moment, he asked me to show him a downstream-nymphing technique. I was rather pleased that he had actually asked me for advice; perhaps it signalled a change in our relationship, after having been war buddies for so long. I intended only to demonstrate the method, but I hooked a fish while I was showing it to him. A terrific silence followed.

If I had wanted to console him I could have reminded him that, just around the corner, he would be redeemed. My moment of despair was on its way: At some point, sometime soon, I would look up and everyone but me would be catching fish. The day was near when a client would complain to me that the fish were too small; that he had had better fishing last year, with another guide. I would have to struggle for the words to right my keeled boat. In times like those, it would help me to remember that our good friend, a respected veteran guide, once went for six straight days without being able to get his client a single fish.

In my darkest moment I will look at the mountains, breathe the fresh air, and try to find more patience for the fly fisher whose line falls on the water in a pile of loose loops. I will remind myself that there are worse places to be standing, and worse jobs, and sadder lives, and finally, when the fishing collapses all around me, and the fly that I want is not in the box, I will wade out of the water, sit down on the bank, and take off my hat to the river that runs without emotions or expectations, and watch the trout rise undisturbed and free.

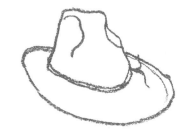

Lappish Knife on Grayling River

Dreamlike, the twilight cast shadows on the Kaitum River. It was July above the arctic circle in Swedish Lapland—a time when, like an unsolved problem, the sun refused to set. I emerged from the mountain birch and willows that guarded the shore along with my guide, Johan, and stepped into ancient waters. The Kaitum's pewter surface was accented by a gray light and I struggled to see what Johan said were rising grayling.

"They're out there," he insisted with a pointed finger. I squinted. "Where?"

"Can't you see them?" he demanded.

His exasperation got on my nerves. I could not see them, but I admitted to seeing them, just so he would leave me alone. Johan stood silent while I watched the river. What I had seen was water that looked like pebbles were raining on it. I guessed that those were rises.

"What kind of fly do you have?" he asked.

"Parachute Adams."

The parachute's white calf-tail top made it more visible. I thought I might have a chance to see it float.

"Do you have a Superpuppa?"

"A what?"

"One of these," he said, pulling a fly from the lamb's wool patch on his vest and holding it out to me.

A dubbed yellow body, a dubbed black head, palmered blue dun hackle all the way from the eye to the bend in the barb, on a size 14 hook. A small, unassuming pattern that I had never heard of. It was supposed to imitate the caddis pupae.

"I don't have one."

"Well, you should. It's the only fly that works," he said as he hooked the fly back onto the wool on his vest.

I now felt a full six thousand miles from home. The only way out of the area was by the helicopter we had flown in on, the only way back to camp was in the motorboat captained by Johan, and the only fly that reportedly caught fish was stuck to a patch of wool three feet away.

I tried the aggressive, but charming, approach.

"Cough it up," I said, smiling and reaching toward him with palm held skyward.

Johan, puzzled by my English, but more by my attitude, stammered, then rallied.

"I only have one. It is the only one left. I can't give it to you."

"I can trade you for it if you like."

"What do you have?" he asked, stepping closer as I snapped open my fly box. He was amazed by the number of flies I carried, but not amazed enough to trade with me for the Superpuppa.

"Do you have any American leaders?" he asked.

I had pocketsfull. We agreed that a package of 5X leader would be exchanged for the Superpuppa.

Johan climbed the bank and disappeared into the brush, heading downstream to fish.

"What an asshole," I thought.

Left alone in a rushing river of arctic cold water that threatened to sweep me into the Baltic with every slippery step, I dug my wading staff down deep and found my footing. I had been in the company of men for several days; I was the only female guest in camp. Privacy had been scarce and Johan's disappearance came as a welcome relief. I tied on the Superpuppa in the dim light.

The noise of the river created a kind of silence. The water pushed against my legs and tumbled over sharp, craggy boulders, drowning out the noises of birds, animals, and the fishermen across the river. But the river could not drown the kind of noise my mind made when I finally found myself alone. I thought of the circumstances that had possessed me with the idea of taking this trip.

Adventure had been a part of my past. As a kid I had begged my parents to send me from our home in Long Beach, California, to survival camp in Montana. I wanted to go to the wilderness and see if I could last for two days with only a jacket, matches, pocketknife, hacksaw, and tarp. No sleeping bag. I was twelve. After two weeks of training, camping, and surviving, I made the long-distance call and begged to stay longer. I did not want to go home. The third week, the camp bus left with me on it for a raft trip down the Salmon River. Three weeks that changed my life. I believed I had been given the skills to survive not just in the woods but in the world. Little did I know that survival often required more than a handful of dry matches.

When the letters and the phone calls came from Sweden, I had hesitated. Leaving my three-year-old son at home felt impossible. I had been asked to help organize the first all-women's fly-fishing school in Sweden, and then to go to Lapland to see if the camp there had any potential to attract American fly fishers. My expenses would be covered. It sounded interesting, a chance for adventure.

Over the years, marriage and motherhood had tried to tame me. Fishing and guiding had become a way of staying in touch with the days when no white picket fence threatened to keep my imagination from wandering. So I said "yes" to the voice on the phone. And found myself standing in a river at the top of the world.

I took a few more careful steps into the current and remembered that our party of Swedes, Americans, and Englishmen was holding a contest. When the manager of the camp heard about our competition he lay the prize on the table: a knife crafted by a Lappish artist. The sheath was made of reindeer bone that had been carved with intricate etched designs in black—the signature work of the Lappish. The handle was made of polished birch wood and reindeer bone. If I could catch the biggest grayling of the week, the knife would be mine.

But I was not thinking of the contest when I cast. I thought more about keeping my line out of the brush directly behind me. I thought of how far away home was, how foreign this country was to me, how new this freedom felt. Free. I definitely felt free. The fly line flew out and over the river. I mended the line upstream and waited.

Not seeing or feeling, but knowing, and not knowing how I knew, I set the hook. The weight of a grayling pulled my line down like an anchor and then ran downstream. I tried to follow. In two steps I scraped my waders against sharp rocks, banged my knee, sank up to my chest, and felt the river hit me like a punch.

"No fish is worth drowning for," I told myself as I backed up.

After fifteen hard-fought minutes I pulled closer what had tried to get away. I had forgotten to ask what size grayling they had in Lapland. This was a big fish by trout standards—over eighteen inches, at least. If all the grayling were like this, it would make up for the snide comments fellow fly fishers had made before I left the States. "Grayling are nothing but whitefish with big fins," they had said. "Aren't there any salmon?"

In quiet water, I netted and prepared to release my catch. Strange fish. Ugly and beautiful at the same time. The scales were layered in nice, neat rows along its body like shingles on a roof. I pulled open the dorsal fin. In daylight the purple and red-blue hues are easier to see; at night the dorsal fin looks dark and steely. I let go and the fin folded back on itself like a Japanese fan. Quiet and patient, the grayling rested. I had to revive it before giving it its freedom. For over fifteen years I had practiced catch-and-release. It was a habit.

Above me Johan came crashing through the brush, shouting, "Let me see what you have."

I lifted up the grayling for him to see and lowered it back into the water to unhook. Johan arrived quickly at my side and reached for the grayling, the only guidelike gesture I had witnessed all evening. I thought he was going to do the honors of unhooking and releasing, but instead he unhooked my grayling and, with a swift and audible thump to the head on a nearby rock, executed it.

"What are you doing?" I screamed.

"You will win the knife!" he answered.

"You could have measured it. You didn't have to kill it."

"I don't have a measuring tape."

"But I didn't want to kill it."

Johan, with typical Scandinavian stoicism, ignored my anxious posturing and walked back into the brush holding my lifeless grayling by the gills. I watched the willows shake as he progressed toward the campfire higher up the bank.

Four more grayling were taken by the Superpuppa until the Superpuppa was taken by the birch tree behind me. I had to tug on the line until the leader broke. As I examined the frayed end of my tippet, the boat containing Lars—the Swedish leader of our group—and the others came into sight. I met them at Johan's campfire.

"Well done! Well done!" my companions cheered as I walked into the fire's circle of light. Hand-carved birchwood cups filled with boiled coffee and spiked with vodka were raised in honor of the catch. Forty-seven centimeters was the official measurement. I thanked my companions, and looked at the ground to hide my grin.

Lars spoke to Johan in Swedish while we stared into the fire. It was easy to listen to them converse in their gentle language. I loved the mystery of not knowing what their words meant, and listened instead to the *way* their words were spoken. That was how I had tried to understand my husband when I asked him if he wanted to join me in Sweden, and he said, "You can go."

Traveling back to camp, our boats pushed upstream. The midnight light gave a soft glow to the wilderness around us. Fog hung in low patches over the water. The hills within hiking distance were rounded and worn. Five-hundred-and-twenty-five-million years worn. For centuries, herds of reindeer numbering in the thousands had summered on the tundra, pawing at the nutrient-rich reindeer moss, cropping it loose with their teeth under the watchful eyes of their Lappish masters. The Lapps gave this country color, wearing red, yellow, and blue in geometric patterns on their clothing and hats. Why did they want to stand out from the landscape—their bold colors looking like shouts? Perhaps for as practical a reason as not getting lost from each other in the forest or in a snowstorm. Maybe their lack of camouflage kept them from being swallowed by the earth. There was so much of it there.

It would be forty-five minutes before we reached the dock. One of the British journalists shared the ride with me. Somehow our conversation turned into song. We started singing show tunes from the film *My Fair Lady*. Competing with the roar of the boats' motors, we unabashedly exercised our Broadway lungs. Laughing and singing, arms held out in dramatic gestures toward the river, we changed the words of the song and sang to the grayling:

> People stop and stare
> They don't bother me
> For there's no where else on earth that I would
> rather be.
> Let the time go by
> I don't care if I
> Can be here on the stream where you live.

I could not remember doing anything so silly and spontaneous since college.

The next day Lars, the two British journalists, and I ventured out under a bright blue sky. A rare warmth allowed us to leave our woolen sweaters and heavy jackets on the bank. We were together, and yet alone, as we cast over the river to raise grayling.

The river bottom was more visible in the daylight. Clear, pure water flowed from the Scandinavian mountains for more than six hundred kilometers to the Baltic. We were fishing a section of the longest river system in Sweden, which had not been dammed or seen its waters harvested for hydroelectric plants. No Giardia parasite existed in the intestines of animals in this country, and so unpolluted was the water that it was drinkable without filtering or boiling.

The rocks in the river were large, slippery, and unstable—the most challenging wading I had ever encountered. My wading staff was destroyed by the end of the trip from jamming it between rocks and using it to hang on in the swift, icy current. Some Swedish fishermen, especially the older spin fishermen, anchor their boats in the middle of the river and cast off the bow or stern wearing big orange life jackets. A life jacket seemed like a good idea and I wished I had one.

At lunch, a huge black skillet balanced over a birchwood fire, and the simmering smoked sausage, potatoes, and onions tempted us to stop our manic quest for fish and break for food. Reindeer skins were carried from the boats to keep us from having to sit on the cold ground. Seated around the fire, we ate our lunch. I was sitting next to Lars when he asked, "What are your plans for the future?"

I thought I should have an answer. I wanted to develop my guide service, work on fly-fishing schools for women, get hired for more speaking engagements, but suddenly all of these plans seemed vague and I felt confused.

"I don't know," I answered.

Looking toward the ground I became aware of the micro-world that carpeted it. Dwarf birches, reindeer moss, crowberries, cloudberries, grouseberries, a miniature forest at my feet. This stunted garden, which existed for mile after mile over the Lappish countryside, had a precious ten-week growing period. Its fruits and grasses fed the reindeer, birds, and other animals in a world that only tilted toward the sun a few weeks each year. Nothing could be taken for granted. Life was short.

What was it that I really wanted? Guiding, schools, and speaking engagements were jobs. Was more work going to make me happy? I had a house, a car, a husband, a child, and trout rivers just thirty minutes away in any direction. Where was the dissatisfaction coming from?

The next day a helicopter carried us more than ten miles inland to a lake on which the Lapps allowed fishing rights. We were left at a drop camp to spend two days fishing for char. A guide had joined us and our group had grown to five. We worked together to set up our camp— tents, sleeping bags on reindeer skins, a rubber-raft, and an open fire—then we set off to see if we could catch the four-pound char we had been promised. The journalists paddled the raft across the lake. Lars and I explored the lakeshore on foot. Ahead of me, Lars found an area to fish, and began to cast. I settled nearby and looked for rises.

Reindeer grazed in the distance while fly lines cut through the evening sky in tight loops.

A char-orange sunset hung over us. As I cast I felt Lars watching me and I turned and caught him looking away. I had noticed the small gestures that he made to be certain I was comfortable. He insisted that my tent be pitched on a flat surface, that I have enough warm clothes, that my fly line be clean. When, I wondered, was the last time I felt attracted to another man, or for that matter, attractive?

I began to notice things about him. The slope of his nose, the shape of his ears, the way he looked walking away, that he changed his shirt before dinner. I was afraid that he would not sit next to me at lunch, and afraid that he would sit next to me at lunch. I asked him questions like, "How far are we above the arctic circle?" just so I could hear him talk. And because we did not confess anything with a touch or with a word, I thought we could keep everything safely hidden, even from ourselves.

As our world shrank to the light of the campfire, we healed our fishless day with food and conversation.

The helicopter arrived late the next morning. We waved as it approached as if we thought it might fly by without us. I was not sure I wanted to be picked up. It meant the trip was almost over.

*U*pon my return to the lodge, I made arrangements to take a sauna. Though the sauna was a communal bath, I was not able to shake my American modesty and asked if I could take one alone. With a knowing smile, the camp manager assured me that I could have the sauna to myself.

Any power needed by the camp was created by generators or solar panels. Hot water was made in kettles over wood-fed stoves. The journey to the bathroom required a walk along a path of wooden planks, leading to a row of wooden outhouses. This dependence on matches, wood, and sun gave the camp a greater sense of isolation, and me a greater feeling of independence. The sweet smell of birch-wood smoke was always in the air. It is a seductive perfume.

Birch wood crackled as its fire warmed the sauna water and rocks. To wash, I had been instructed to ladle the warm water over my body. A bucket of cold river water had been brought in to pour over the rocks to create steam. When I got too hot I could douse myself in the cold water as well. In the small, dark chamber I became dazed by the heat. A heat that went all the way through to the soul. It became so warm I could see how a person's modesty might get lost somewhere in the steam. Water was the only thing you desired. Cold water, to keep you from disappearing, to keep you alive.

It occurred to me that I did not miss him—my husband. I thought that I should try to miss him, but longing for him did not exist. I missed my son and that was all. I tossed a ladle of river water onto the rocks; they sizzled as if they were burning. We were a couple with a child, we looked good on the Christmas card, but habit had taken the place of heart. To know this was only part of my discovery. I needed to rediscover the determination of that fearless girl who begged to be sent into the wilderness to sleep in the Montana woods without a sleeping bag. She was the one who could demand that people not kill her dreams. I wanted her to show me how to stand out in primary colors and awaken the flat landscape of my inner life. I tossed another ladle of water over the rocks and I could barely breathe.

The last night arrived, and we sat down to our final meal together in the main lodge. The lodge's exterior had been beaten by the elements and looked brave but wounded. European flags flew from the eave of the roof at the entrance. Inside, it was fresh and bright. The polished birch-wood floor and furniture glowed. The custom was to leave your shoes at the door. A large stone fireplace with a newly lit fire drew guests to the couch in front of it. We suddenly felt civilized.

We began with glasses of dry Italian wine, smoked grayling with dill, and the Swedish caviar, löjrom. The meal had been created of regional favorites: reindeer fillet with lingonberry sauce, boiled potatoes, mushrooms that had been picked just outside camp, fresh salad, and freshly baked bread. For dessert we were served warm cloudberries, picked from the tundra and spooned over vanilla ice cream. Our glasses were filled with Punsch, a traditional Swedish drink made from arrack, a liqueur similar to rum.

Satisfied and tired by our long days under the arctic sun, we were sitting in a comfortable silence, sipping the Punsch, when the award ceremony commenced. A speech by Lars, some good-hearted teasing by the British, and the knife was placed in my hands. My fishing friends raised their glasses in congratulation.

*T*he agent at the ticket counter handed me my boarding pass.

"Do you think you'll ever come back?" Lars asked as my luggage disappeared down the airline's conveyor belt. For eight hours I flew above the Atlantic suspended between the shores of choice.

*W*eeks later, in my living room, I pulled the Lappish knife from its sheath: the blade honed by hand, the cutting edge curved in the shape of a grayling's dorsal fin. In its shiny surface I could see the future rising in front of me. I put the knife back in its sheath and pushed down until I heard the distinctive click of it locking into place. In the months that followed, as I sat in my lawyer's office sorting out the difficulties of leaving a man who did not want to be left, and not knowing if I would ever again see the man I had not wanted to leave, the knife hung on the mantel keeping the days in reindeer country alive so that I would know I had not been dreaming when, at twilight on a grayling river, I had found the me who was missing, and she had come home.

The Best Day

$\mathcal{T}$he streets of Bozeman, Montana, from May through September, waken to the sight of trailered Mackenzie River boats squeaking and bouncing behind their owners' vehicles. It is the fishing season, and the guides are on their way to clients and rivers.

I do not have a boat, since I am a walk/wade guide, but I join my peers in the early-morning exercises of picking up lunches and getting to the fly shop on time. We meet at Safeway in the cookie-and-chip aisle; sunglasses, held by straps, dangle from our necks as we study the shelves looking like misplaced librarians. We swap greetings and ask, "Where are you headed?" We wait patiently behind each other at the Exxon station, one hand on the steering wheel, the other holding a cup of coffee. The season's routine is so well worn into my guide psyche that it comes back to haunt me in mid-December at four in the morning. I wake up panicked, having dreamed I had a guide trip, and could not find the fly shop, and had forgotten to order sandwiches.

I like the routine. It is a pattern that gives me something to count on, because after I shake hands with new clients, the rest of the day is unpredictable. We begin by speaking to each other with a certain politeness that, like a sheet, drapes over the shapes and contours of our personalities.

"Where are you from? How long have you been fly fishing? What kind of gear do you have? Do you have any flies?"

"Where are you from? How long have you been guiding? Where will we be going today? Do you think we'll catch anything?"

By 8:30 A.M. the parking places in front of the fly shops are vacant. The last truck with hatted clients and guide has entered Main Street traffic and headed either east or west, toward a river in either direction.

Although I generally prefer the traditional fly-shop pickup, on this morning I met my clients at their lodge. After driving for two hours, the last six miles over a dusty dirt road, I arrived. I tossed my empty coffee cup onto the floor in the backseat, and stuffed the McDonald's Egg

McMuffin wrappers under the front seat, and stepped out to meet my client and his family. I reached to shake his hand. A firm grip grabbed back. He was strong and solidly built, like a box with rounded corners. His wife, an attractive woman brimming with confidence, was pleased that her husband had found an instructor for himself and the children. She had other plans for the day, and she smiled as she waved good-bye with an arm heavily weighted by turquoise bracelets. The teenage boy, long-legged and awkward, spoiled with privilege, looked over the top of my head and around me, searching for something to free him from his self-consciousness. The daughter, a seven-year-old, had her mother's personality and decided that the children's hike was more interesting to her than a woman in a cowboy hat who was going to take people fishing.

Although it maintained a humble exterior, the dude ranch was much more than a corral-and-bunkhouse affair. A chef with a tall white hat prepared gourmet meals and rang an antique triangle the size of a wagon wheel to announce meals. The massage sign-up sheet was posted on an easel by the front desk; the fax and copy machine room was to the left. Trail rides were as predictable as a bus schedule. Square dancing was offered at least once a week. Cowboys and other local talent sang after dinner. Events were so well organized and attended that my client's son decided he could fit in his fly-casting lesson between the breakfast ride and the nature walk. The father would take his guided trip after lunch.

The son and I stood in front of the ranch's casting pond. Stray children who had not signed up for a program that morning tossed spinning lures with worms, hoping to catch one of the five-pound stocked trout that cruised the shoreline. Amused by our presence, they harassed my self-conscious teenage client by pointing out to him that he could not catch anything with the piece of yarn I had tied onto the end of his leader. They informed me that I was an adult and therefore not allowed to fish there. They buzzed around us for more than a half-hour, until some-one mercifully called to them from the front porch of the lodge, and they all ran off like a herd of frightened deer.

"Let me show you how to stop the rod at the top of the casting stroke." I took the boy's hand to demonstrate, and felt like I had touched an electric fence.

"I get it," he stammered.

His wrist continued to roll forward and backward off a stiff forearm; the line, predictably, landed in a pile in front of us. I gently took his arm and pulled his elbow back to his side, then tried to show him how to maximize the movement in his elbow and minimize the movement in his wrist.

"I get it."

His arm jutted higher and higher to the sky with each stroke, until I had to reach up and quietly guide his arm back down from the clouds.

"Oh, I know."

He began to push the rod like he was moving a stan-dard shift from first gear to second and back again. I told him to accelerate the movement to a stop, but not to jerk or punch it to the stop.

"Oh, I get it."

The harder he tried, the worse everything became.

"Let's try a roll-cast," I suggested. He liked the roll-cast. The forceful, chopping motion needed to make it work suited him perfectly.

"Can I put a fly on now?" he asked after a five-pounder rose to examine the pink yarn that was now rolling out in perfect formation across the pond. I hesitated, knowing that as soon as we started to catch fish the casting lesson would be over, but I did not want him to lose his enthusiasm so I said "yes."

We plotted together. I had him begin by casting and stripping a Woolly Bugger. Sometimes I would cast for him, then let him work the fly back to the bank. Trout followed the black Woolly Bugger, darting and snapping at its tail, but they were not really interested. We cast a Royal Humpy and watched patiently while trout went up to look at it, then moved away. I spotted a bag of dog chow someone had left leaning up against a nearby tree and realized what it was for.

"Here, toss these out there." I gave the boy a handful. The pellets brought trout from all corners.

"Cool," he said.

I chummed with the pellets, he stripped a Prince Nymph through the piranha water, and we caught one of those stocked five-pound rainbows. The wide-bodied trout headed for right field and gave my student a good lesson in line control and reeling. Being a teenager, he had a certain level of coolness to maintain, but a light of inspiration seemed to have turned on in his head and he reeled in the trout with trembling hands. After we unhooked and put back the fish it was time for lunch. We both tossed dog food and watched the trout rise before leaving for the main lodge.

"I caught one!" he announced proudly to his parents. "It was huge. I was the only one who caught one this morning."

His parents beamed. As if his son were not standing there, the father asked, "So, how is he? Is he any good?"

A face that asked for lenience peered from behind his father's shoulder.

"If he wants to get any better he'll have to practice, but as long as he's having fun and is interested the rest will follow."

Everyone seemed happy with the diagnosis. The chef rang the triangle and I was invited to lunch.

Several guests seemed to think it was exotic that I had been imported to give private casting lessons, and began asking how they could get their own. The family I was working with was pleased with the attention and made a point of talking about their son's success that morning. He quietly complained that they should not make such a big deal about it.

After lunch, the father emerged from the family's cabin looking like a model for the Orvis catalog—the fishing vest was stiff with newness. All of the correct hardware hung from his chest, like tools in a tool shed. The felt on his wading boots was as white as snow. A handcrafted Brodin net swung on his back. The line was shiny from lack of use. The rod had never caught a fish. The reel was on backward, but I turned it around.

"Wow," I said, "you look great!"

His wife took a photo.

His casting lesson took place on the lawn behind the main lodge since I did not have the courage to face the children's pond and its resident hecklers. He was calm and easygoing. His bear-sized hands and round body did not suggest that he had had anything to do with the fathering of his nervous stringbean-shaped son.

"What you said about pushing on the grip with my thumb when I cast forward really helps," he said.

He was one of those rare people who connects with a fly rod almost immediately. It just looked right from the beginning, and he was charmed by the way line seemed to magically flow above his silhouette on the lawn.

"I could just stand here all day and cast," he said, smiling.

We did not have to travel far to the water, since a perfectly sweet little creek ran along the last six miles of the rutted dirt road I had traveled that morning. The warmth of the midday sun raised the water temperature enough to awaken the rainbows and cutthroats that slumbered, and the caddis were dancing their erratic dance, here and there, over the water.

Even in hip waders we were overdressed for the ankle-deep creek, but we stepped in, waded out to the middle, and faced upstream. My client cast a size 14 elk hair caddis, and I pointed to the places it should land.

"Oh, hey! Look at that," he said when the first fish struck his fly. He was truly awed. He had never fly fished before. The second time a trout struck my fisherman connected. His shouts of surprise and joy rang up and down the creek and we happily reeled in a sparkling, eight-inch wild rainbow.

"Isn't that beautiful," he said softly, and every trout after that was beautiful, incredible, amazing, fantastic. A little brookie took the fly and I held it so my fisherman could see the blue rings around the bright orange spots.

"That's the prettiest thing I've ever seen," he said with sincerity.

To be with someone who was able to treasure the moment the way he did made me feel like I was exploring fly fishing for the first time. I showed him how to keep his fly from dragging, how to fish the deeper pools, how to fish a seam line. He was absorbed by the whys and the hows and the executions. And the fish, whether six inches or ten, were praised like precious stones.

In the late afternoon, about the time the skin begins to feel a little sore from a fresh sunburn, my client stopped fishing. His shoulders dropped and he paused to look at the water, the trees, and finally at me.

"I have to tell you something," he said. "This has been one of the best days of my life. The reason I'm telling you this is because I wasn't supposed to be here right now. I haven't felt this good in years. I've been very sick. The doctors didn't think I was going to make it, I wasn't sure I was going to make it, but I've been well since last fall and everything is fine now. My wife gave me this equipment because I've always wanted to fly fish, and this trip is kind of a celebration for our family. So, I just want to tell you that because this really has been one of the best days of my life."

I could not speak. I looked into his eyes and nodded. He smiled at me and cast again. We left the creek only after hearing the triangle ringing in the distance.

His wife, who was waiting on the front porch of their cabin, embraced him and asked how he had done. "Fantastic, absolutely fantastic." The children followed him inside, interrupting each other to tell him what they had done that day. I could see that the dark cloud that had hung over them for so long had passed, and they were finally able to enjoy something as simple as being a family on vacation.

Down the dirt road my Jeep bounced over ruts and rocks as I followed the creek that had given us "fantastic," "beautiful," "amazing" trout. The next day I would resume my routine. Sandwiches at Safeway, gas at Exxon, coffee in a styrofoam cup, new fishermen to meet.

"Where do you think we'll go? Will we catch anything?"

I will put them in my car and drive them east to a river they have dreamed about all year. We will dress, choose flies, step into the water, and begin the day. I will think of my fisherman who had his best day ever and not wish for anything more.

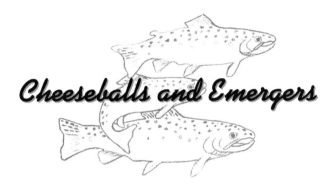

Cheeseballs and Emergers

I became a fly fisher not because of aesthetics, or passion, or politics, or trend, but because when I was growing up we had fly rods in the garage. When we went camping my father always packed the fly rods in the car, handing them to us when we came in sight of water. My brother Tom and I tossed Royal Wulffs as big as wine corks over the lakes and rivers of our youth without questioning our parents' style of fishing or type of gear. We never caught anything—we had not yet been schooled in the art. We just fooled around and we were content.

During our travels, my brother and I observed other kids' and families' fishing methods. We watched from a distance as cheeseballs were carefully rolled and pressed onto hooks, and worms were pinched from styrofoam containers and speared into contorted S shapes. We had seen the big red-and-white plastic bubbles that went "splat" when they hit the water and floated like buoys. It all looked strange to us. We were curious, and when we had the chance, we tried to cast spinning rods and chuck shiny Mepps lures over the water with the strength, grace, and skill that our peers did.

Our attempts were fruitless and I must confess that to this day I cannot coordinate the pressing and releasing of the button on a spinning rod. I am hopeless. With all my might I wind up and throw forward, and the line always stops short and slingshots the metal lure back toward my face, where it dangles in front of my nose ringing like a wind chime. Either that or I let go too soon, and the lure lands behind me in the water.

Although I have heard stories and have witnessed firsthand that food, animals, and animal by-products on the end of the hook are effective, I have always stood by the familiar—what has worked for me. I never thought I would feel inclined to exchange my fly rod for a spinning rod. If I am honest, my lack of skill influenced my preference more than anything. I have been in situations where I allowed my imagination to wander, and I wondered if my luck would turn luckier if I had a spinning rod with something shiny and smelly and twirling at the end of the line.

As a fly-fishing guide, I have been coached to avoid impure thoughts of augmenting or altering the natural condition of a reputable fly. If God had wanted us to fish with worms, they would grow on the backs of elk or in the necks of chickens. But just once, I allowed my imagination to go too far. I am not proud of what I did, but I will share my story like someone on a talk show who publicly confesses a perversion or a crime. I am willing to do this because my experience taught me something about myself, something I did not realize I needed to know.

My partner in crime was a client whom I had taught and guided for nearly three years. Lynn always looked forward to her annual family vacation in Montana with her husband and two children. Her husband liked to fish too, but he insisted on looking after the kids and shooed her off the lodge's front porch so she could take a few days to fish, undisturbed by the demands of the family.

Over the years Lynn and I had become friends. She had let me critique her casting, I had let her critique my divorce. I would tell her to stop popping the cast forward, she would tell me to contact her husband's law firm if I needed a second opinion. We still post photos of each other's children on our refrigerators.

Because I knew she would like the adventure, and because I wanted her to catch some large fish, I had planned a special trip for Lynn that summer. I wanted to show her new and beautiful surroundings and help her catch lots of fish. She has always had the patience, temperament, and appreciation for the sport that make her a real fly fisher at heart. She loves everything about being in the outdoors and on a river, and so, when the fishing is slow and conditions are tough, she is the one a guide will make bargains with God for.

"Please dear God, just one fish. Just give Lynn one nice fish. We'll take whatever you can give us, and we'll put it back. Just one fish and I won't wish for anything more. I promise to be satisfied with just one."

That day we drove for an hour before we reached the trailhead. I was shocked at the number of cars in the parking lot—more than twenty. Surely they did not all belong to anglers. I rationalized away my worries with the thought that the cars belonged to day-hikers or backcountry campers. We donned our gear, stuffed our lunches in our backpacks, locked the car, and were on our way.

The trail was steep, and we took short breaks to rest. At one point we stopped to let a fishing party on horseback pass. The outfitter wore a sweat-stained cowboy hat and a neutral expression. He nodded in recognition of our presence, took a drag on his cigarette, and exhaled. The smoke wafted over his shoulder, sparking images of western towns, bars, and John Wayne. The riders sat slouched and relaxed, their rods tied securely to their saddles. They turned politely to smile one at a time and then returned to study the spaces between their horses' ears. Except for a few snorts from the animals, the group passed in silence. Women with fly rods do not have the shock value they once did. Taking out my mental notepad, I wrote down, "Men on horseback look comfortable. Will be fresh by time they get to creek. Will have more time to fish. Women on foot will be tired. Get phone number of outfitter off horse trailer in parking lot."

Lynn and I continued on the hike, admiring the Indian paintbrush, harebells, and fireweed. A doe and her spotted twins let us photograph them before they shied away into the timber. At the top of the ridge we stopped to take in the view of the valley we had just come from. We could see that the trail ahead dropped and would deliver us to our destination on the other side, where large cutthroat trout were rumored to sip and suck and cooperate with anyone who tossed an elk hair caddis, hopper, or Royal Wulff in front of them. We happily marched on.

After twenty more minutes Lynn asked, "How much farther?" I had already begun to worry about the same thing, but for other reasons. I was feeling a little guilty because I had neglected to tell Lynn that I had never fished this place before. I had seen enough slide shows and read enough magazine articles to feel I had been there before, but the truth was, I had not. Scary feelings rushed in and intensified when the river finally came into sight with fishermen elbow-to-elbow along its banks.

Fly fishermen stood staring and casting into the slow, quiet waters that wound in oxbow curves through the open valley. Fly lines bright and wet were flying in the mid-morning light. It looked like a casting clinic.

The group of horseback-riding fishermen was among the crowd. The outfitter sat in the grass watching over his dudes, puffs of smoke trailing toward the sky. He turned and stared at us, and then the entire creek gazed our way. There is nothing wrong when people notice you making an entrance. In fact, it can be flattering. But fishermen do not like crowds, and I felt that we had walked in on a private conversation, and should quietly turn around and go back where we had come from. Maybe they only looked up to make sure we were not bears, but collectively we all knew the fishing spot was getting crowded. In order to set up along the river as from the others as possible, Lynn and I would have to walk by and around all the men who were there.

My confidence began heading down the trail and I began to question myself: "Maybe I should hike up another two miles. I remember someone said it was good there. Why are all these people here if it's better up there? Why didn't I fish this first before bringing a client?"

I continued to beat myself up until Lynn interrupted me. "Well, we came to a popular place. There must some fish here."

She was right about that, and I tried to put the possibility of success back into the day.

Smiling, head held high, I stepped into the meadow acting like I did it all the time. Lynn followed me past the fishing-in-progress.

"Hello. Good morning. Hi. Hello. Hi. Good morning."

As we offered our greetings, I noticed one important fact. No one was catching anything.

I have pride, but sometimes I am able to abandon my poker face and ask, "How's the fishing?" The man who answered this time wore a hat that looked like he had sat on it, and a fishing vest appropriately decorated with surgical instruments for clipping, snipping, and extracting. With a look of frustration and sorrow, he shook his head and said, "I fished all day yesterday and since early this morning, and I can't get anything to work. You can see them feeding on something really small. They sit on the bottom and then come up to something tiny. The fish are huge. Look at them. I can't figure it out. I thought if I came early when it was cooler. . . . Maybe we need some cloud cover. Maybe I should try something big. I've tried everything. It's tough. Just really tough."

As he spoke a large cutthroat rose quietly to the surface, sipped, and sank down. "See!" said the fisherman, dropping his shoulders and sounding like a kid whose building blocks had just been knocked over by his older brother. "See that!"

An uncomfortable silence followed. We looked at the river and back at our feet. Resigned to his tough luck he said, "You have a good day. I hope you can figure it out. I sure can't."

We trudged past the tenth gentleman in a half-mile stretch. Cutthroats lined the edges of the creek. Where there was a boulder or a depression, there was a fish. Every riffle was home to at least one native. The sight of these large trout feeding and resting quietly within reach had me thinking. I felt my confidence returning. I had a feeling that we could get one to take.

I began by tying on a size 18 sparkle dun for Lynn. Minutes later I had her switch to a size 20. After observing what looked like a plague of grasshoppers, I had her switch to a hopper pattern. Then we changed to a beetle, an ant, a Griffith Gnat, Adams, Parachute Adams, Royal Wulff, Royal Humpy, Elk Hair Caddis, and back to beetle. The dry-fly patterns failed, so I switched to the wet-fly patterns. We sank pheasant tail nymphs, midge pupae, and caddis larvae, all in assorted sizes and colors. In exasperation I tied on a black Woolly Bugger and had Lynn strip it so close to a fish that it bumped it on the nose. The cutthroat calmly moved over to let the fly go by. Trout kept rising to an emerging insect we could neither see nor identify. I began to make bargains with God: "Please dear God, just give Lynn one. . . . "

After two hours of fishing we had not caught a thing. Neither had anyone else on the creek. The sun was high and hot, the wind still. I was feeling tense, and when the buzzing of flies began to sound like lawn mowers, I decided to break for lunch.

We sat on a boulder overlooking a deep pool where several large cutthroats rested. Occasionally, one would shimmy over to a new place on the creek bottom. It was like looking at an aquarium in a doctor's office. Everyone was waiting. Watching and waiting.

We ate our turkey-and-Swiss sandwiches quietly and continued to study our targets below. Out of curiosity, I pinched a piece of bread from my sandwich and flicked it into the pool. As soon as it hit the water I felt a little strange, as if I had thrown a pop can out of my car window. As I reflected on this, a dark shadow rose from the bottom, sipped in the bread, and dove back down.

"Lynn," I said quietly. "Did you see that?"

"Do it again," she prodded.

Again the bread crumbs brought the hard-sell cutthroats up to the surface. I quickly looked around to see if anyone was watching. I needed a simple hook that would hold the bread. I grabbed a small midge pattern called a Brassie and quickly pressed the bread around it. The moment ran away with me.

"Do you think I should do this?" I asked Lynn.

Lynn nodded. "See if it works," she encouraged.

I flipped the breaded hook into the pool. As it hit the water, the bread fell off the hook, and two cutthroats came up and ate the crumbs. I was delighted and bothered at the same time. This was not fly fishing. This was not really fishing at all, but playing with the fish. This was not supposed to be fun, but it *was* fun.

"I need something that will stay on the hook," I said.

Suddenly, a childhood memory flickered into focus. *Cheese. Cheeseballs.*

I opened my partially eaten sandwich and pulled out the cheese. I carefully pinched off a piece, squeezed it onto the hook, and offered it to the trout below.

All eyes were upon us as we netted the eighteen-inch cutthroat. Downstream the sound of someone spooling his reel pierced the silence that followed the excitement we had caused. It was the frustrated fly fisherman we had met

earlier, and he was walking toward us. Soon he stood inno-
cently and quietly beside us.

"What'd ya catch it on."

Taking the opportunity to burn in Hell I replied, "A
Prince Nymph."

Trying to avoid any evidence, I even lied about the fly
I had stuck the cheese to. Lynn watched our conversation
like someone watching the ball at a tennis match.

"I have a few more if you'd like to try one."

I removed one from my vest and held it out to him with
a smile.

"No. No thanks. I've tried one of those already. How
did you fish it?"

"Downstream."

"Okay. Well, I'll just have to keep trying."

After he left, Lynn and I packed up the remains of our
lunch and moved a little farther away to avoid the prying
stares from our audience. She caught two more cutthroats
on the cheeseball fly. I checked out the mood of the fishermen along the bank. Nobody else had caught a fish.
Some fishermen had left for other parts of the creek.

Oddly enough, after we had had our fun I did not feel
like the fish we caught counted. What was the matter with
me? It was just fishing, we had both gotten a big laugh out
of it, wasn't that the whole point? Did I take myself too
seriously? What was it that made me feel so defeated?

We would never forget the looks of disbelief on the fly
fishers up and down the creek when they saw us catching
fish, but that day I learned that, for me, there is something

truly satisfying about catching fish on flies. The cheese-balls had kept us entertained, but the experience just was not the same. I had become a fly fisher by habit, but on that trip I emerged a *true* fly fisher. To this day I am more willing to take my defeats as I deserve them, and the cheese stays in the sandwich.

Split Cane

During the Yellowstone Park fires of '88, when we thought we were previewing the end of the world, I got an emergency phone call from a neighbor in West Yellowstone. The winds had shifted. I was urged to come immediately and rescue any valuables from my father's cabin. There was not much time. Fire threatened to burn down the door.

I thought our neighbor, fueled by the excitement the fires had created over the past month, had exaggerated how close the fire was coming to the cabin, but it was the event of the decade, and I had finally gotten an invitation, so while the Jeep engine ran I tossed my infant son into the arms of a friend and left Bozeman for the two-hour drive south.

Smoke and haze had hung over the state of Montana since July when the first lightning bolt had set the park on fire. Hundreds of miles from the fire, ash fell on houses and lawns. People with allergies and asthma called their doctors. Parents took their kids to tailgate parties, complete with picnic baskets, where like drive-in moviegoers, they parked within viewing distance, sat in their cars, and watched. At night we watched on television and learned how many acres had burned. In coffee shops and on street corners people lamented, "The park is gone. Never in our lifetime will we see it the way it was. Somebody should have stopped it."

When I reached Fan Creek, a crowd of firefighters was holding conference in the turnout area, while the blades of the helicopters spun. A thundercloud of smoke billowed off mountains in the distance.

Twenty minutes from West Yellowstone, the landscape was blackened and smoking. The fire had jumped Highway 191, burning both sides for miles. Cresting the hill that leads out of the canyon and into the valley, I could see volcanic columns of a forest fire exploding. Fire, ash, and smoke were everywhere.

The town of West Yellowstone looked like it was under siege. Gone were the usual August visitors walking around with Cokes wondering if they might see bears. The U.S. Army had sent troops. Busloads of young men in camouflage and army fatigues walked the streets. I locked my doors and accelerated the eight miles out of town to my dad's place.

What should I save? I had not thought to rent a trailer to haul furniture away, so I would have to be selective. My dad's instructions were to get the fishing gear and the artwork, and then look around and decide if there was anything else worth saving.

Finding the fishing gear and piling it in the car was easy. My father had left all the rods loose; tips, butts, and midsections were stacked in the corner of a back bedroom like tepee poles. The canvas bag of Hardy reels was under the kitchen counter. The other canvas bag, full of fly boxes, lines, and miscellaneous tackle, was next to it. I pulled watercolors, sketches, and framed flies off living room, bedroom, and bathroom walls, wrapped them in bath towels, and then repacked the car, placing the fly rods that had lost their rod tubes years ago carefully on top.

After that I stood on the porch, looked at the cabin, and thought, "What am I really doing here? What am I here to save?"

The fly rods were not particularly special. The Fenwick and Sage graphite rods, the Hardy reels, and the lines could have been replaced—with the exception of the fiberglass Fenwicks that, I admit, I felt sentimental about. The artwork was nice, but new art could be found to take its place. My father wanted me to save the cabin by saving the fishing gear and a few pictures. After that I could leave the key in the door. Funny what it all boiled down to.

I had been asked the question before, but never thought I would be acting on it. "If you were home alone and your house was on fire, and you could get out alive, and you had the chance to save only one thing, what would it be?"

"Photographs," I had answered.

So I went back into the cabin to look for one photograph in particular.

Photographs are proof that you existed. They are footnotes that trigger the memory of an entire experience. They let you look into the faces of your parents as children.

I found a kitchen drawer full of candids. One was of my younger sister Carrie and brother Tim as they helped each other land a trout from the pond down the road. Carrie must have been seven, Tim five. There was one of their mother (my father's second wife) kneeling in front of a string of fish that she and my father had caught before their divorce, and before we became catch-and-release people.

A black-and-white I had taken of my dad and our neighbor shows them smoking cigars after a successful trip to the Madison River; my older brother Tom throws a snowball off the porch during a July snowstorm in another.

My father's third wife poses with a steelhead on a trip they took to Alaska, and there is a photo of her two children holding my infant son at his baptism.

Someone took a picture of a moose that frequented the meadow next to the cabin. There were dozens more of family members holding fish; their faces full of pride and happiness during those days when a fishing trip rejuvenated us and gave us a reprieve from the difficulties we had with each other and the world, for we were a diverse and complicated group: a California extended family that sought the healing waters of rivers.

With a nostalgic sigh I grabbed the rest of the loose photographs, slipped them into a grocery bag, and continued the search.

Balanced on the second shelf of a bookcase was the framed photograph I was looking for. The one of my great-grandfather, Sidney Miller. Next to his photo rested two of his Pfleuger reels from the twenties. To me, these items were worth the whole place. Sidney had had a particularly good day of fishing. He stood in his backyard holding one end of a stringer of nineteen trout, while the fence post held the other end. Trout, from ten to sixteen inches, hung like laundry. He smiled modestly. His hip boots looked clumsy, since the straps had been released and the tops of the boots bagged at his knees. The all-important fishing hat was pulled back at a rakish angle so that shadow did not hide his face.

If the fence was a neighborly one of four-foot height, then Sidney was a tall man—over six feet, like my father, his grandson. When I studied his face, I saw my father's nose, the same nose my older brother has, and the same one that I look at each morning in the mirror.

The photo was still in its original thin, brown frame, with a paper sticker on the back that said L. H. JORUD COMMERCIAL PHOTOGRAPHER, LANGAN DRUG CO., HELENA, MONTANA. Helena was where Sidney lived. It was a photo taken sometime in the thirties when he may have been in his early fifties. Despite the smoldering cigarette in his left hand, Sidney looked like a strong, healthy man. The only history I know of him is what my father remembers. Sidney was a kind and easygoing person who bought my father ice cream. He became a widower at an early age when my Irish great-grandmother, Loretta Finnerty, died and left behind two small children.

I think of the grief. Mothers, grandmothers, and great-grandmothers have died at young ages on both sides of my family. Generations of children have grown up without their mothers. I try to find it in my great-grandfather's face. I see someone who has been hit hard, but made a resolution to go on.

That's all I know of him. But in this photo I can see that he liked to fish, and that connection draws me to his image as if I know him. Why that seems so important, I am not sure. I guess I expect the past to somehow confirm who I am, and reveal some kind of hidden message that will foretell the future. I am not sure if the photograph of my great-grandfather does all of that, but it is a comfort, and I can see, at least, that our passion runs in the family.

The reels were tarnished but seemed to be in working condition. Some cleaning and oiling were in order, and I began to wonder what it would be like to use them some day. I knew I could not stand to see these antiques on the reel seats of modern, shiny graphite rods. The best thing would be to put them on a split cane rod, except I did not have one. Well, I decided, one day I would have to get one.

Satisfied that I had saved things of value, I put the reels and the photograph on the passenger's seat next to me, checked to make sure nothing would fall on or crush the rods in the back, and into the late afternoon of a thousand campfires I drove my great-grandfather and his grandson's memories home.

*T*he rod case at Dan Bailey's in Livingston, Montana, holds split cane rods. Some are new, some are old. The old ones have been brought in by their current owners to sell on commission. The prices for split cane rods, old or new, were between $700 and $1,500. I wanted to see them, but I was shy about asking. One of the salesmen saw me staring into the rod case, came over, and opened the glass door.

"You like bamboo?" he asked.

"I've never cast one before. What are they like?"

"They're slow," he answered like a warning.

Split cane rods were made from bamboo, a plant that is related to the grass family but grows in clusters, like trees. The stem of the bamboo was split then put back together—not the way it was, but stronger and more flexible than before. You could learn something from a split cane rod.

I had heard that split cane rods were magic rods. They came alive in your hand. They were art and history and hours of craftsmanship and skill, designed by men who engineered them in thousandths of an inch, in secret. They were wrapped in silk thread and varnished with special finishes so rare and fine that the recipe cannot be duplicated today. Split cane was as personal a choice as choosing a mate. I got the feeling the salesman had not heard about split cane.

"You want to look at one of these?" he asked in a tone that said, if I did not, he had other things to do.

"I'd like to try this one." I pointed at a walnut-colored cane rod with a price tag of $1,500.

The salesman took the rod out, put it together, and waved it in front of him like a divining rod.

"One of the guides in town has to sell this. You picked the best one of the bunch. You know what this is? This is a Payne. You know anything about Payne?"

I knew that Ed Payne had studied the rod-making of H. L. Leonard, who made the Stradivarius of split cane rods. That Payne had taught his son, Jim, the art of split cane rod-building at an early age, and because his son's talent was so obvious and precious he forbade him to play strenuous sports in case he should injure his hands. Payne rods were exceptional.

The rod I was about to meet was dark, flame-tempered cane, built circa 1916 by Jim Payne.

"Here, you gotta try it," said the salesman, and he held it out for me to hold.

The worn cork grip, colored from use, found its way to my hand. I felt like I had just been seated on the back of an American Saddle Bred that was going to rack away with me at high speed. I waved the rod, not really knowing what this move was supposed to prove, and experienced an unexpected dizziness, a shortness of breath. Each wave of the rod made me feel more and more light-headed. I thought I was going to faint.

"Here, I'm afraid I'm going to break it." I quickly handed the rod to the salesman.

"You can't break it," he said, trying to hand it back to me.

"No. Thanks anyway. It's very nice. I'll come back later."

Forgetting what else I needed, I went out the door desperate for fresh air.

One afternoon in late June I walked the banks of a spring creek south of Livingston. Livingston, where my father's mother had been born in 1901. Erie Montana McLaren. I thought of her, knowing that the Absaroka Mountains that lorded over the Paradise Valley looked the way she had seen them more than eighty years before. I wondered if my grandmother had known anything about this creek, if it had held any interest for her.

Pale morning duns rode the current, their wings held up like praying hands, as if they contemplated a merciful god who might allow their wings to dry so they could take flight before a large rainbow trout sipped them down to an untimely end.

Slurp.

One disappeared.

Snap, slurp, slurp, snap
Four more gone.

Silvery flashes of rainbows turning, and dark wavering trout shadows in the riffles and pools, held my attention. Like a crouching cat poised to attack birds on a lawn, I kneeled on the bank to watch.

I did not hear the two fishermen who walked up behind me, but I felt their presence and turned. I greeted them and explained that I was not fishing and would move if they wanted to get in the water. One of the fishermen was a photographer who was there taking photos of his older friend, Ted. Ted was a strong personality seasoned by time. He wore hip boots and khaki.

"Guess how old he is," the photographer asked.

"Forty-nine?" I said, politely picking a number twenty years younger than I suspected.

"You aren't going to believe this. He's eighty-five!"

You have to be careful how you react to such news. Great excitement over an outstanding age could be misunderstood, as in, "Shouldn't you be dead by now?"

"I hope I'm fishing here when I'm eighty-five," I answered.

"Ted comes here every year just to fish the pale morning dun hatch."

I wondered why the photographer spoke for Ted. "Ted," I asked, "How's the fishing been?"

"Unreal. Absolutely great. Look there, another one." He pointed to a fading rise ring.

"Where's your rod?" he continued.

"I left it. I just wanted to come look at the creek. I'm going to fish it tomorrow."

"I like to do that too. Just watch the creek," Ted said knowingly.

By then he had seated himself on a bench made from a board off the side of an old barn. The photographer danced around us, his camera clicking and whurring. Ted and I watched the trout rise and tried to ignore the photographer.

"Look at that, look at those fish rise," said Ted, and it was then that I noticed he was pointing at the trout with a split cane rod. We watched the creek some more and then he said, "Why don't you take my rod and fish?"

"No thank you," I stammered. "I can't."

"Why not?" asked Ted.

"I've never cast a split cane before. I'm not sure I should fish, I haven't paid a rod fee and. . . ."

"Do you know what kind of rod that is?" said the photographer, "It's a Payne! It's an original. This is a chance of a lifetime!"

I gripped the edge of the bench. Just hearing the name made me feel a little off-center. Ted turned to me and offered the rod again. He spoke, and it sounded as though he were talking to me underwater, "Go ahead, I'd like to see you fish with it."

The innocent, honey-colored split cane rod rolled into my hand.

"I met Payne before he died. Go on, fish," Ted commanded as he waved me toward the creek.

With a size 6X leader, and a size 18 Harrop PMD no-hackle tied to the end of a 7½-foot Payne split cane rod, I walked, knees weak, toward the water.

My greatest worry was that I would dishonor the rod by casting poorly. I knew split cane had a different action than graphite. I knew I would have to slow down my casting stroke. I knew that I would have to listen to the rod and let it tell me what it needed. I lifted the tip with thirty feet of line and began to cast.

Everything I had heard was true. Split cane is magic. It lives.

I did not just cast the rod, I had a conversation with it. We became a team. It was like a well-bred horse. I had to be careful not to spook it with sudden jerky movements; I had to pay attention to its mood. The rod turned the line over smoothly and I watched the leader and fly land. The drift required a mend and, to my surprise, with a simple roll of the tip the soft-action split cane mended my line upstream without causing the fly to skip, backhop, or make a ripple. By the third cast, I had hooked an eighteen-inch rainbow. The cane bowed gracefully like the neck of a swan as I played the trout. The photographer's camera clicked.

Ted was delighted.

"Fish some more," he offered as I spooled the line after releasing the trout and walked toward him.

"I really appreciate that, but I need to be going."

It was not exactly true, but it was not exactly untrue either. The moment was the way I wanted to leave it:

a memory of catching a rainbow on a spring creek in Montana with a Payne rod, beneath my grandmother's mountains.

I was waiting at the Bozeman airport. As soon as he stepped off the plane, my life would change. My life had already changed, but this was the definitive moment when plans became reality and the act of being would begin. I was afraid. The big glass windows vibrated with the sound of the engines. I could not decide where to stand. My arms were heavy. I decided without deciding to stand back near the wall, where I could see the whole room and everyone in it.

People began walking through the gate. People wearing nice new clothes and carrying packages. They smiled. I smiled. What if I did not recognize him. What if he walked by me by accident. What if . . . and suddenly he was there.

Women should not be so in love. It is embarrassing. You compromise too much when you are in love. You give everything away, and then you regret it. People see how foolish you are. They want to tell you things, things about life, about disappointments and failures. Theirs and yours. They are certain you will be sorry. They have been there, and like mature adults, they have gotten over it. You need to get over it and behave yourself. You are a grown woman living in the nineties; you are not supposed to need a man. You are supposed to be strong on your own because a man tries to take your strength away and you have to be ready so you can live without him. You should practice living without him even when you are with him, just in case.

"Can't you find someone who lives closer?" my oldest brother had asked.

"Maybe he could take an apartment in town, so you could get to know him better and you'd each have your own place in case it doesn't work out," my friend had suggested.

"What kind of person is he? How long was he married? How many kids does he have? Have you had enough time? Do you know this guy?" my father had questioned.

Trying to explain to people how in love I was with a man I had spent two weeks with made me sound like an adolescent, not a grown woman who, I thought, should sound more aloof, more in control. Each time I tried to tell someone how I had never felt this way before, how he and I connected, how I knew we were meant for each other, I could sense their suspicion and their nausea. So I quit talking about it. I knew. They would see. Everything would be fine.

It must have looked like a compulsive thing to do. Separate from a husband one month and start living with another man the next. Maybe it looked desperate.

"Can't she be on her own for a while?" "Can't he wait for her to get on her feet?" "There hasn't been enough time." "Is he really moving in?"

Lars flew in that night from Sweden. America's newest immigrant. His leap over the Atlantic was our leap of faith.

We had not seen each other for over a year. We had arranged for our new life together by fax and phone. We did not need more time. Life was too short for those kinds of careful plans.

Tears, the kind you shed when babies are born, washed over our cheeks. Words did not form. The room emptied and we were still there. I was handed a gift. I opened the case. It was a split cane rod. "Because," he said, "you always wanted one." Amber-colored, with burgundy silk windings. Magic. The rod-maker's signature suddenly blurred in my vision along with something about . . . with love from Lars. For a long time I only knew his shoulder and a clean white shirt that would have to be washed.

I cast the silk line Lars had given me. It was his, but he wanted me to have it for the split cane. It made a scratchy sound when it moved across the rod tip. I was glad that it was olive green and not one of the plastic bubblegum colors that modern lines come in. My great-grandfather's Pfleuger looked at home on the rosewood reel seat. I fished a Gim River dun, a delicate olive dry, a fly Lars had designed and tied.

We were on Slough Creek in Yellowstone National Park. From several different vantage points you could see large sections of charcoal forest, scars from the fires of '88. Luckily, our neighbor had been wrong. Our cabin outside West Yellowstone had not burned. But it was hot, like that

August four years earlier, and the summer sun had torched the green meadow to cornflake yellow. Large cutthroats held in the deepest pools and under the banks. Some kept to the riffles, and let the bubbling water tickle their gills and backs.

I cast the split cane slowly and smoothly. The line rolled out and landed quietly. I cast again. The casting was as interesting as the fishing. The rod and I were friends.

The fly disappeared into the mouth of a large cutthroat. I had to wait before I set the hook. Cutthroats are like that. They are not like rainbows or browns. They do not rush your dry. They have another personality. Sometimes they drift backward to examine your offering more closely; they think it over, and try to decide. When the decision is in your favor you wait a beat or two before you set the hook.

It is rumored that cutthroat are stupid fish. Maybe they got that reputation because they are so slow, like split cane. I think they are misunderstood. They are an old fish. Wise. They have been here longer than we have. They have something we do not have. Time.

I set the hook. The split cane bowed and bounced with life. My hand turned where my great-grandfather's hand had turned, and I listened to the reel click as the silk line was spooled. The fish, frightened and determined, fought against the line. As it was pulled toward the net it turned the water to flame with its red cheeks and slashed throat. Split cane lifted it up and over the net's rim to safety. It did not know that after its fight it would be free.

In the beginning, nothing had seemed simple about the plans for my new life with Lars except that we wanted to be together. What I learned in our struggle to reach each other was that it takes courage to get through the kind of fire that takes your home or your heart. Courage is difficult, like split cane. Being difficult makes it worth something.

I unhooked and held the cutthroat in the water. Across the high country meadow Lars called my name and hurried toward me with his camera. If within the next hour or the next day, tragedy or sorrow invaded our lives, I would always have this moment when all was well, and we had each other. I looked toward Lars and lifted up the trout for him to see, and smiled with all the joy I felt.

Winter's Dream

First, I had to get a boat. I had been down to the lake and seen two rowboats, one that looked like it had an owner, the other like it did not. The boat that looked abandoned was full of water and old leaves. It had two roughed-up wooden oars that had been left in the oarlocks, paddles pointing toward the sky like mergansers' feet when they dive for fish. Bail out the water and it would be perfect. I wondered if I could find the owners, and if they would rent it to me for the summer.

I wanted to take my eight-year-old son fishing. All winter I had been creating and re-creating our days together on Lake Myssjön in a rowboat. I believed that the morning would be chilly, but the steady sun would peek through the boughs of the fir and pine forest of the Swedish countryside while we hiked the path ten minutes from our house to the water. I would carry most of the gear, but he would carry the net and his life jacket. I would have packed sandwiches and milk, and a thermos of coffee. It was a scene that I conjured up, and that added excitement to my annual preparations for the journey to Sweden, my husband's country.

Part of the scene was the absence of my husband, Lars. I wanted this time with Peter, alone. Lars agreed to help me find and speak to the owner of the boat.

I do not speak Swedish, yet. I do not mind. I watch the body language and listen to the soft sounds of Swedish as it floats off the tongues of everyone around me. I understand what they are talking about, I can usually follow the conversation, but I cannot answer. Not having to answer is a great relief. I do not have to answer the phone. I do not have to answer personal questions. I do not have to answer the mail. I do not have to answer. It does not bother me.

I knew when Lars was finally speaking to someone who knew something about the boat because, when he pointed in the direction of the lake, the man nodded. I also knew when they were discussing the terms of the deal. Lars smiled and looked very pleased, almost grateful, so I knew it had been settled. He turned to me and translated.

"The fishing board owns the boat and you are welcome to use it anytime, no charge. They want you to remember to tie it back up when you're finished."

"*Tack så mycket!*" I said to the man.

I had a boat.

I thought I would go the next morning, but I did not. The idea of taking Peter fishing suddenly felt different from the warm, sunny picture I had painted all winter. What if he did not like it? What if I tried to instruct him and instead started to nag him? What if he felt the tension and said something irritating like, "I already know how to do it, Mom!" I wished I had not wished so hard for a perfect day. I needed to rethink the scene and make it less perfect, then I would not be crabby and disappointed if things did not go the way I had planned. I did not want either of us to not have a good time. I had to rethink my motivation for taking Peter fishing.

What did I expect, or what did I want from the experience? I wanted to take Peter fishing because I wanted to give him a childhood fishing experience. I wanted to have a memory of fishing with Peter when he was eight years old. I wanted to be together with him. I secretly wanted him to like fishing, fishing with me. I wanted to be the hero if he liked it, but not the villain if he did not. If I truly wanted to be together with him then I would need to drop idyllic expectations and simply be together with him.

So I decided that when the weather was right we would go fishing. I would go to have an interesting time with my eight-year-old that included fishing. I would go knowing that the line might get tangled and knotted, that the lures might get knocked into the water, that he might get bored after an hour. I would go knowing that these are the things that can happen when you go fishing with a child, and I would make an effort not to spoil our fun with my expectations.

About a week later, in the middle of a sunny afternoon, the time struck me as right. Warm, no wind. We had already eaten lunch, so there were no sandwiches to make. To remove some of the structure of my earlier plans felt right. It would be a spontaneous excursion and it would develop on its own.

Lars pulled out the gear we would need from the shed. We had decided that spin fishing would be easier for Peter to learn. Although I had learned to fish on a fly rod, I had been older. There was a bump in my conscience about this, because I wanted to keep up the family tradition of fly fishing, but it would not be at the expense of fun. Fly casting would come later when we were both ready for it.

We each took a spin-casting lesson from Lars since I could barely throw a spinning outfit myself. The lures looked like spare car parts compared to the delicate flies I had spent most of my life casting. I had no idea what kind of knots you needed to connect swivels. And no taper to the leader—just yards of monofilament to throw out and reel in. I would have to guess at technique. No mending, no drag to worry about. Check the hook from time to time and make sure there is no grass stuck to it. This could be interesting. Peter's mother, catch-and-release apostle, professional fly-fishing instructor and guide, taking him spin fishing.

The oars made satisfying creaks as we pulled away from shore. Peter sat in the stern wearing his green rubber boots, jeans, T-shirt, and bright orange life vest. The old brown felt hat that Lars had given him had barely left his head since it had been put there three weeks earlier. The hat had been shrunk by the rain of many fishing trips when Lars had traveled with it to Lapland, England, and the United States. Its warped brim gave it a well-loved look. Peter liked the hat because it made him feel like Indiana Jones.

Peter was always dressing up to be someone he admired. There had been a space stage when he wore a fleece jumper that looked like a space suit. He wore it day after day, even in 100-degree weather when sweat trickled down his cheeks. I could not persuade him to take it off. He wanted to be Spock, then Captain Hook, then a policeman. He wanted to be King Tut, and Dr. Allen Grant from *Jurassic Park*. The Indiana Jones impersonation had been going strong all summer. It fit with his desire to travel to Egypt to find a tomb full of gold. I had been made to promise that someday he could go to Cairo and to the Valley of the Kings so he could see the great pyramids. On the world map in his room, we could see that Sweden was closer to Egypt than Montana was. In a way, he was already halfway there.

As he explored his heroes, I had to wonder who he might become. What subject would drive his curiosity, what person would inspire him, how would his life be different from mine? Different. For some reason one of the first questions people ask me when they meet Peter is, "Does he fly fish yet?" I see why they think it might come naturally to him, since he is surrounded by fly fishers, professional and otherwise. I hope that he can see his choices, and that his world is not limited to trout and grayling rivers. The Nile sounds like a good river to me.

I explained to Peter that he must not stand up in the boat or lean too far over the side. He followed my directions and sat patiently in the middle of his seat, holding the spinning rod, smiling. A happy child. That was what I really wanted. I wanted that smile.

I looked at the lake to see where to begin. A river tells you by the way the water pushes over rocks or flattens into quiet eddies where you should and should not send your fly. A lake is a different story. As with the Swedish language I had not yet learned, I could not understand this lake. I put my fishing mind to work. Oxygen, food, and shelter are what fish require, I had told my students. So they must require these in a lake as well. The shore was full of insects, mosquitoes, caddis, and damselflies. "Stay close to shore," I thought. Later, I learned that a lake is like one big carnivorous pool of fish eating other fish. The small fish eat the insects near shore, while the big fish eat the small fish. In a way I had been right, but I still had a lot to learn about lake fishing.

I rowed the boat outside the line of cattails that grew fifty feet into the lake. If the boat was too close, the lure would get stuck in the grass and reeds; if it was too far away, I would not know where to tell Peter to cast. It helped when I saw perch rising to something minute. I took the boat over to their feast and told Peter to cast into the middle of it.

Peter was eager and ready. The rod was too big for him but he managed to hold on by splitting his fingers around the reel stem. I came up with a way for him to remember the steps. Step one: Press the line against the rod with the index finger. Step two: Open the bail. Step three: Tip the rod back and cast forward, releasing the line at the stop. It worked. I did not have to nag him. To help I just had to say, "You forgot step one," or "two," or "three."

I rowed up and down the shoreline, experimenting with different angles, wondering when or if a fish would take. I had promised myself not to expect anything. Not catching fish, like not winning at checkers or cards, was part of life, something to be suffered through, even at eight, but I did not feel like being a witness to suffering right then. I wanted a perch to take Peter's lure so that he could begin to see why I liked fishing so much. Perhaps I was trying to lead him to an understanding.

"Mom, I think I've got something!"

Every time before, the lure had been stuck on some grass, but this time the tip of the rod bounced with life and I knew that he had caught a fish.

"Keep the rod tip up and reel! Good, Peter! Good work!"

I pulled in the oars and watched. The perch popped up out of the water from Peter's enthusiastic reeling. It was fast-forwarded upward. Its mouth, held open by the hooks, gave it a horrified look, as if it knew it would be forced to swallow the rod tip.

"Hold it! Stop reeling. Now swing the fish over here."

A small perch swung and hit me in the face like a wet mop.

"Ahhhhhh!" I screamed, which caused Peter to erupt into a fit of laughter.

The perch wiggled as I grabbed hold of it. It was hooked in the mouth by all three barbs. I realized I did not have pliers to pinch them down or pull them out. How had I forgotten them? I tried to untangle the perch from the barbs the way I untangled leader knots. Pushing and pulling, going forward and backing out. I could not undo the hooks, and the fish had been out of the water too long. In the canvas bag was the priest that Lars had tucked in at the last minute.

"You may need this," he had said.

I had never used a priest before.

The last time I had killed a fish had been fifteen years earlier. The incentive had been an angry breakup with a man. I had left him after a weekend of the hopelessly bad communication that had been the theme of our six-month relationship. He always sent me beautiful cards, when he was out of town, and in them he wrote about how much he missed me, but when we were together he never even offered to hold my hand. I went fishing and decided to catch a fish and fix it for myself. I yanked hard on the brown trout when he took my grasshopper pattern, and rapped his head on a nearby rock. At home I stuffed him with lemons, onions, and butter, and baked him in foil at 350° for thirty minutes. I ate half of the fish that evening; the other half stayed in the refrigerator until it started to smell and I had to throw it out. I vowed never to kill another trout, especially not over a man.

The priest had a simple wooden handle on one end, and a heavy brass cylindrical knob on the other. Just by looking at it you knew it was made for hitting. This particular model was supposed to be used over the head of a pike, but I could not bring myself to follow the local custom of killing a perch by pushing a thumb under its throat and snapping its head back for a quick and painless death.

"Peter, I can't get the hooks out and I can't let the fish suffer."

I took the priest with authority, and tried to make the event a simple and soon-forgotten one. The sound of three solid thumps, like someone knocking on the side of the boat, echoed across the lake.

"Is it dead?" he asked.

Not looking at my son, I studied the perch to make sure I had not botched the job. The first blow left it looking insulted; the second blow stunned it and it convulsed in shivers; after the third blow it lay still. I watched as the life force within that ten-inch perch evaporated like mist at noon. Its eyes glazed over the moment it lost its spirit to the winds. An unexpected feeling of loss set in. I had killed something. It bothered me.

"Yes, it's dead now."

Without ceremony I began to wrench the hooks out of its mouth. I did not want to let Peter know how sorry I was. I wanted him to feel that this was natural and normal and a part of life.

"Oh, Wakan Tanka, Master of Life, thank you for giving us this fish," said Peter as he looked toward the sky.

I stopped tearing the hooks away and looked at my child. Lars was a great admirer and follower of Native Americans and their history. He had talked to Peter many nights over dinner about the ways of the Native Americans—how they worshiped Wakan Tanka, and thanked Wakan Tanka immediately after killing the game that would feed them. Peter's little prayer had taken me by surprise.

"Do you think God is mad at us? Aren't we supposed to put the fish back?" he added.

The Great Master of Life had given us the fish, but God was mad. Peter was confused and so was I. He had been raised in a family of fly fishers that went as far back as his great-great-grandfather. He had heard about catch-and-release all his life, and thought it was against the law to kill a fish. Who was he to believe? I was not prepared for this conversation.

"You are supposed to put the trout back because, if all of the people who wanted them killed them, there wouldn't be any left in the rivers. We can take the perch because there are a lot of them in the lake, and not many people fish for them here."

I was not sure this answer would hold up, but it was the best I could do.

"Can I touch it?"

Peter reached for his fish and held it with a mixture of suspicion and admiration.

"Let's put him in the bail bucket to keep him wet," I said.

We had been fishing for almost two hours. But neither of us felt like going home. Peter wanted to row, and I had been stalling on an answer to his request. I hesitated because I knew the oars were too heavy for him and we would lose control of the boat. I had not dreamed that Peter would want to row the boat. I had been a guide too long. I gave him the oars.

The boat spun around in circles in one direction and then the other. Peter dug so deeply into the water that he had to stand up to pull the oars back. I showed him how to angle the paddles through the surface so that he could stay seated when he pulled. We wove in and out of the cattails and then spun around some more in open water. He laughed because he was having fun. I laughed because he was having fun. His arms got tired and it was time for me to row us back to shore.

We tied up the boat and up the trail we walked, slapping at the mosquitoes. I carried most of the gear while Peter carried the net, his life jacket, and the fish. We were tired and moving slowly when we came in sight of the house and saw Lars waving to us from the kitchen window. Peter yelled to him, "I got one!" and held the perch up for him to see.

I had something too. I had the boat and I had the summer and, most importantly, I had the little boy to share it with. My winter dream had come true, better than planned.